THERE WERE GIANTS IN THE EARTH IN THOSE DAYS

Also by Bob Mitchell

Antichrist and the Third Temple

Rome, Babylon the Great and Europe

Antichrist, The Vatican and the Great Deception

Signs of the End

The Messiah Code

The Post Tribulation Rapture of the Church

A COLLECTION OF VARIOUS REPORTS REGARDING THE DISCOVERY OF THE REMAINS OF GIANT HUMAN BEINGS

There were giants in the earth in those days; and also after that, when the sons of God came in unto the daughters of men, and they bare children to them, the same became mighty men which were of old, men of renown.

Genesis 6:4
The Holy Bible

INTRODUCTION

As children, we enjoyed being told stories of giants that lived in the sky or in secret dens, in caves or long forgotten ruined castles. giants, who terrorized the poor, defenceless human beings unlucky enough to encounter them.

But what if the children's tales of gigantic sized beings had a grain of truth hidden within their pages?

The author of the book of Genesis chapter 6 verse 4 when writing about the days in which the patriarch Noah and his family lived tells us "There were giants in the earth in those days." Is this true? Or ancient Hebrew fiction?

We later read of King Og whose army the Hebrews encountered and fought on their way to the promised land after leaving Egypt in the Exodus (Numbers 21:33).

Og was a big guy, by all accounts. His bed, we are told, was 9 cubits long and 4 cubits wide. If that means nothing to you, a cubit was approximately 18 inches. Therefore his bed was 13 and a half feet long by 6 feet wide. Even if we calculate the bed was slightly longer than King Og we may still be forgiven for imagining a man who, in his socks, stood around 12 feet tall.

When David, the young shepherd boy, fought Goliath he stepped onto the battlefield facing a man of around 9 feet 6 inches tall. Goliath had 4 brothers who, it would appear, were not much smaller.

The ancient Hebrew book of Enoch also describes powerful beings called the watchers who came from heaven and had sexual relations with women creating hybrids of great strength and height.

The Bible itself goes on to describe the different tribes of giants (the supposed offspring of the Watchers) the Hebrews encountered on their journeys.

For instance, as they were faced with the opportunity to enter the Promised land, Moses sent 12 spies into the land to reconnoiter the area.
On their return, instead of being thrilled with the possibility of an early entry and conquest of the land they returned terrified and deflated stating:

Numbers 13:26-33

And they went and came to Moses, and to Aaron, and to all the congregation of the children of Israel, unto the wilderness of Paran, to Kadesh; and brought back word unto them, and unto all the congregation, and shewed them the fruit of the land. And they told him, and said, We came unto the land whither thou sentest us, and surely it floweth with milk and honey; and this is the fruit of it. Nevertheless the people be strong that dwell in the land, and the cities are walled, and very great: and moreover we saw the children of Anak there. The Amalekites dwell in the land of the south: and the Hittites, and the Jebusites, and the Amorites, dwell in the mountains: and the Canaanites dwell by the sea, and by the coast of Jordan. And Caleb stilled the people before Moses, and said, Let us go up at once, and possess it; for we are well able to overcome it. But the men that went up with him said, We be not able to go up against the people; for they are stronger than we. And they brought up an evil report of the land which they had searched unto the children of Israel, saying, The land, through which we have gone to search it, is a land that eateth up the inhabitants thereof; and all the people that we saw in it are men of a great stature. And there we saw the giants, the sons of Anak, which come of the giants: and we were in our own sight as grasshoppers, and so we were in their sight.

To say "We looked like grasshoppers in their sight" may be true or an exaggeration. But the fact of the story is, the spies had entered the land (an heroic and risky thing to do in the first place) and had seen inhabitants that were of such stature, any hope of an easy conquest totally evaporated, leaving them despondent and extremely fearful of any encounter with the people they had witnessed.

The Greeks also wrote of the Titans, divine beings of great strength who descended to earth and ruled for many years.

Cultures from around the world have legends of giants who terrorized the population or warred against them until the giants were finally wiped out.

But where are the remains of the giants? Could it be that as each successive civilization grew the graves of the giants were lost?

America is a relatively new land. Indeed the United States is only 341 years old.

As settlers slowly wound their way through a treacherous, unknown land, hoping to put down roots and live a peaceful life in the new country, they dug into the rich earth to build, to plant, to establish a presence. And as they did so, they unearthed the bones of a hitherto race of people unknown to them. A race of giants, the indigenous American Indians however, knew well through the stories their ancestors passed down while sitting around the camp fires. Stories of battles with a race of giants so fierce many braves were lost. Until one day there were no more giants. The wars were over and peace descended.

Then the white man came and as he did, the truth of

the red man's tales came to the surface and the newspapers of the time reported the discoveries. Here are those eyewitness reports of the remains of some of the descendants of the giants who once ruled the earth.

This book is by no means exhaustive. But may be used as an interesting book of reference and a stimulus for further study.

REMAINS OF
ANCIENT
GIANTS

CLEVELAND HERALD, SEPTEMBER 10, 1845
A GIANT EXHUMED.

We are informed on the most reliable authority that a person in Franklin county, Tennessee, while digging a well, a few weeks since, found a human skeleton, at the depth of fifty feet, which measures eighteen feet in length. The immense frame was entire with an unimportant exception in one of the extremities. It has been visited by several of the principal members of the medical faculty in Nashville, and pronounced unequivocally, by all, the skeleton of a huge man. The bone of the thigh measured five feet; and it was computed that the height of the living man, making the proper allowance for muscles, must have been at least twenty feet. The finder had been offered eight thousand dollars for it, but had determined not to sell it any price until first exhibiting it for twelve months. He is now having the different parts wired together for this purpose. These unwritten records of the men and animals of other ages, that are from time to time dug out of the bowels of the earth, put conjecture to confusion, and almost surpass imagination itself.— Madison Banner.

STROUDSBURG, PENNSYLVANIA
JEFFERSONIAN REPUBLICAN, OCTOBER 2, 1845

A STORY OF A GIANT.

In exhuming of late the remains of so many wonderfully large animals unknown to the present age, it has been supposed that the ancient race of men must have been correspondingly large. At length we have something to sustain the doctrine. The Madison Banner states on the most reliable authority, that a person in Franklin county, Tennessee, while digging a well, a few weeks since, found a human skeleton, at the depth of fifty feet, which measures eighteen feet in length. The immense frame was entire with an unimportant exception in one of the legs. It has been visited by several of the principal members of the medical faculty in Nashville, and pronounced unequivocally, by all, the skeleton of a huge man. The bone of the thigh measured five feet; and it was computed that the height of the living man, making the proper allowance for muscles, must have been at least twenty feet. The finder has been offered eight thousand dollars for it, but had determined not to sell it at any price until exhibiting it for twelve months. He is now having the different parts wired together for this purpose. These unwritten records of the men and animals of other ages, that are often from time to time dug out of the bowels of the earth, put conjecture to confusion, and almost surpass imagination itself. History informs us that the Emperor Maximum was 8 feet 6 inches in height. In the reign of Claudius a man was brought from Arabia 9 feet 9 inches tall. John Middleton, of Lancashire, England, was 9 feet 3 inches, and Cotter, the Irish Giant, 8 feet 7 inches. But our American skeleton, if we have really found such a one, will throw all other Giants in the shade.

THE BOSTON MEDICAL AND SURGICAL JOURNAL, JUNE 19, 1856
MEDICAL INTELLIGENCE

Western Giants in their Slumber.—The Burlington (Iowa) State Gazette says that while some workmen were engaged in excavating for the cellar of Governor Grimes's new building, on the corner of Maine and Valley streets, they came upon an arched vault some ten feet square, which, on being opened, was found to contain eight human skeletons of gigantic proportions. The walls of the vault were about fourteen inches thick, well laid up with cement or indestructible mortar. The vault is about six feet deep from the base to the arch. The skeletons are in a good state of preservation, and we venture to say are the largest human remains ever found, being a little over eight feet long.--Calendar (Hartford).

THE NEW YORK TIMES, NOVEMBER 21, 1856
SKELETON OF A GIANT FOUND.

A day or two since, some workmen engaged in subsoiling the grounds of Sheriff WICKHAN, at his vineyard in East Wheeling, came across a human skeleton. Although much decayed, there was little difficulty in identifying it, by placing the bones, which could not have belonged to others than a human body, in their original position. The impression made by the skeleton in the earth, and the skeleton itself, were measured by the Sheriff and a brother in the craft locale, both of whom were prepared to swear that it was ten feet nine inches in length. Its jaws and teeth were almost as large as those of a horse. The bones are to be seen at the Sheriff's office. – Wheeling Times.

BALLOU'S MONTHLY DOLLAR MAGAZINE, AUGUST 1860
"THERE WERE GIANTS IN THOSE DAYS."

The theory that humanity of the antediluvian period existed in forms which would now be considered colossal, has found many adherents among scientific men. A fossil skeleton of enormous size, recently discovered near Abbeville, France, was regarded as a proof of this theory. A Dr. Fullratt, of Berlin, has more recently found other remains of some antediluvian giant in the village of Guiten, near the junction of the Rhine and Dussal. The discovery has created quite a flutter among the wise men of Germany, and a commission has been formed for digging in divers places of the same geological formation as that wherein the giant skeleton was found.

THE NEW YORK TIMES, DECEMBER 25, 1868
From the Sank Rapids (Minn.) Sentinel, Dec. 18.

Day before yesterday, while the quarrymen employed by the Sank Rapids Water Power Company were engaged in quarrying rock for the dam which is being erected across the Mississippi, at this place, found imbedded in the solid granite rock the remains of a human being of gigantic status. About seven feet below the surface of the ground, and about three feet and a half beneath the upper stratum of rock, the remains were found imbedded in sand, which evidently had been placed in the quadrangular grave which had been dug out of the rock to receive the last remains of this antediluvian giant. The grave was twelve feet in length, four feet wide, and about three feet in depth, and is to-day at least two feet below the present level of the river. The remains are completely petrified, and are of gigantic dimensions. The head is massive, measuring thirty-one and one-half inches in circumference, but low in the front, and very flat on top. The Femur measures twenty-six and a quarter inches, and the Fibula twenty-five and a half, while the body is equally long in proportion. From the crown of the head to the sole of the foot, the length is ten feet nine and a half inches. The giant must have weighed at least 900 pounds when covered with a reasonable amount of flesh. The petrified remains, and there is nothing left but the naked bones, now weigh 304¼ pounds. The thumb and fingers of the left hand, and the left foot from the ankle to the toes are gone; but all the other parts are perfect. Over the sepulchre of the unknown dead was placed a large, flat limestone rock that remained perfectly separated from the surrounding granite rock.

OHIO DEMOCRAT, JANUARY 14, 1870
CARDIFF GIANT UNDONE WITH AN ENORMOUS IRON HELMET

On Tuesday morning last, while Mr. William Thompson, assisted by Mr. Robert R. Smith, was engaged in making an excavation near the house of the former, about half a mile north of West Hickory, preparatory to erecting a derrick, they exhumed an enormous helmet of iron, which was corroded with rust.
Further digging brought to light a sword, which

measured nine feet in length. Curiosity incited them to enlarge the hole, and after some little time they discovered the bones of two enormous feet. Following up the "lead" they had so unexpectedly struck, in a few hours' time they had unearthed the well-preserved remains of an enormous giant, belonging to a species of the human family, which probably inhabited this and other parts of the world, at the time of which the Bible speaks when it says: "And there were giants in those days."

The helmet is said to be of the shape of those among the ruins of Nineveh. The bones of the skeleton are a remarkable white. The teeth are all in their places and all of extraordinary size. These relics have been taken to Tionesta where they are visited by large numbers of people daily.

When his "giantship" was in the flesh he must have stood eighteen feet tall in his stockings. These remarkable relics will be shipped to New York early next week. The joints of the skeleton are now being glued together. These remains were found about twelve feet under the surface of a mound, which had been thrown up probably centuries ago, and which was not more than three feet above the level of the ground around it.

BROADSIDE ADVERTISEMENT PUBLISHED AT SARATOGA SPRINGS, NY, AUGUST 10, 1870
$5000 REWARD!

$5,000 Reward for a piece of the same material as the Cardiff Giant. We make the above offer to any man, as we know there is nothing of any kind in the country.

Again, we will give every Visitor ONE DOLLAR when, after a careful examination believes the Cardiff Giant to be a Humbug.

C. O. GOTT. Business Manager.

Phila. Street, near Post Office.

Below will be found an interesting letter from Prof. Wilson, of Saratoga Springs:

SARATOGA SPRINGS, AUG. 6, 1870

DEAR SIR:—I have visited the "Cardiff Giant" several times, and examined it carefully, both by daylight and by gaslight, and am free to confess, that to me the monster stone man is a mystery.

If it is a veritable work of art, I cannot understand why any sculptor, possessing the skill to produce so perfect a specimen of statuary, could have consented to place his subject in such an unartistical grotesque position. Again, I cannot understand how, by any known art, the whole surface of the body could possibly be made to exhibit so perfectly the perspiratory and oil tubes, visible in all parts, not only to the naked eye, but specially so under a microscope.

Again, if it is a veritable work of art, and as some claim, a very recent one, I defy any man to show how the abrasion of the limbs, on one side, manifestly produced by the action of the elements, could possibly be imitated by artificial means.

That it is a humbug, an imposition, I cannot stultify myself sufficiently to believe. If it is a petrifaction, as some honestly think, to what race did the monster belong? I leave the old fellow, as thousands have, with the question of an inquirer, "What is it?"

H. A. WILSON.

Saratoga Springs, Aug. 10th, 1870.

[Note: Hiram A. Wilson (1812-1893) was an educator, Christian missionary, and secretary of the Saratoga County Bible Society known for his Christian piety.--]

CHICKASAWBA
REMAINS OF GIANTS FOUND IN ARKANSAS

HUMAN SKELETONS UNEARTHED EIGHT AND
TEN FEET IN HEIGHT

RELICS OF A FORMER RACE.

The statements which we make below, and the facts detailed, are so strange and almost incredible, and so like the many roorbacks and canards that have from time to time appeared in the press of Europe and America, that we premise them with the declaration that they are strictly true, and that we have not exaggerated what we have seen, one iota. With this much as preface, we will proceed to our story.

CHICASAWBA
Two miles west of Barfield Point, in Arkansas County, Ark., on the east bank of the lovely stream called Pemiscot river, stands an Indian mound, some twenty-five feet high and about an acre in area at the top. This mound is called Chichasawba, and from it the high and beautiful country surrounding it, some 12 square miles in area, derives its name— Chchasawba. The mound derives its name from Chickasawba, a chief of the Shawnee tribe, who lived, died, and was buried there. This chief was one of the last race of hunters who lived in that beautiful region

and who once peopled it quite thickly—for Indians, we mean. [...] Aunt Kitty Williams, who now resides there, relates that Chickasawba would frequently bring in for sale as much as twenty gallons of pure honey in deerskins bags slung to his back. He was always a friend to the whites, a man of gigantic stature and herculean strength. [...] A number of years ago, making an excavation into or near the foot of Chickasawba's mound, a portion of a GIGANTIC HUMAN SKELETON was found. The men who were digging, becoming interested, unearthed the entire skeleton and from measurements given us by reliable parties the frame of the man to whom it belonged could not have been less than eight or nine feet in height. Under the skull, which slipped easily over the head of our informant (who, we will here state, is one of our best citizens), was found a peculiarly shaped earthen jar, resembling nothing in the way of Indian pottery, which has before been seen by them. It was exactly the shape of the round-bodied, long necked carafes or water-decanters, a specimen of which may be seen on Gaston's dining table. The material of which the vase was made was a peculiar kind of clay and the workmanship was very fine. The belly or body of it was ornamented with figures or hieroglyphs consisting of a correct delineation of human hands, parallel to each other, open, palms outward, and running up and down the vase, the wrists to the base and the fingers toward the neck. On either side of these hands were tibae or thigh bones, also correctly delineated, running around the vases. There were other things found with the skeleton, but this is all that our informant remembers. Since that time, wherever an excavation has been made in the Chickasawba county in the neighborhood of the mound SIMILAR SKELETONS have been found and under the skull of every one were found similar funeral vases, almost exactly like the one described. There are now in this city several of the vases and portions of the huge skeletons. One of the editors of the Appeal yesterday measured a thigh bone, which is fully three feet long. The thigh and shin bones, together with the bones of the foot, stood up in a proper position in a physician's office in this city, measured five feet in height and show the body to which the leg belonged to have been from nine to ten feet in height. At Beaufort's Landing, near Barfield, in digging a deep ditch, a skeleton was dug up: the leg of which measured between five and six feet in length, and other bones in proportion. In a very few days we hope to be able to lay before our readers accurate measurement and descriptions of the portions of skeletons now in the city and of the artifacts found in the graves. It is not a matter of doubt that these are HUMAN REMAINS, but of a long extinct race—a race which flourished, lived, and died many centuries ago, in those days told of in Scripture. ("And there were Giants in those days.") It was Sir Hans Sloan, we believe, who first put forth the theory that the gigantic bones found in various parts of the old worlds were not human remains, this so ill according with the popular ideas and superstitions about giants, was considered the rankest sort of heresy at the time; but Cuvier, the great anatomist, proved them, in almost every instance, to be portions of the fossils of mammoths, megatheriums, mastodons, etc. The bones that he examined, however, were those of such apocryphal skeletons as that found in Sicily in the early part of the eighteenth century, three hundred feet long, of "Bucart," found at Valence in 1705, thirty feet high, of the "chevalier Rinson," found at Rouen in 1509. Within the past century there have been numerous well-attested instances of giants over eight feet in height. [...] With these individual instances before us, and knowing the enormous size of almost the entire population of portions of Kentucky, we do not need to be disciples of Henrion, the French academician (who believed Adam was one hundred and twenty-live feet high, Noah twenty-seven feet, Moses twenty feet, and so on down to the era of Christ when the decrease stopped) to be convinced that the race of aboriginal men who built the large mounds in various parts of the country were of gigantic frame and enormous stature.

Dunnville, Ontario: There is not the slightest doubt that the remains of a lost city are on this farm. At various times within the past years, the remains of mud houses with their chimneys had been found and there are dozens of pits of a similar kind to that just unearthed, though much smaller, in the place which has been discovered before, though the fact has not been made public hitherto. The remains of a blacksmith's shop, containing two tons of charcoal and various implements, were turned up a few months ago.

The farm, which consists of 150 acres, has been cultivated for nearly a century and was covered with a thick growth of pine, so that it must have been ages ago since the remains were deposited there. The skulls of the skeletons are of an enormous size and all manner of shapes, about half as large again as are now to be seen. The teeth in most of them are still in an almost perfect state of preservation, though they soon fall out when exposed to the air.

It is supposed that there is gold or silver in large quantities to be found in the premises, as mineral rods have invariably, when tested, pointed to a certain spot and a few yards from where the last batch of skeletons was found directly under the apple tree. Some large shells, supposed to have been used for holding water, which were also found in the pit, were almost petrified. There is no doubt that if there is a scheme of exploration carried on thoroughly, the result would be highly interesting. A good deal of excitement exists in the neighborhood, and many visitors call at the farm daily.

The skulls and bones of the giants are fast disappearing, being taken away by curiosity hunters. It is the intention of Mr. Fredinburg to cover the pit up very soon. The pit is ghastly in the extreme. The farm is skirted on the north by the Grand River. The pit is close to the banks, but marks are there to show where the gold or silver treasure is supposed to be under. From the appearance of the skulls, it would seem that their possessors died a violent death, as many of them were broken and dented.

The axes are shaped like tomahawks, small, but keen, instruments. The beads are all of stone and of all sizes and shapes. The pipes are not unlike in shape the cutty pipe, and several of them are engraved with dogs' heads. They have not lost their virtue for smoking. Some people profess to believe that the locality of the Fredinburg farm was formerly an Indian burial place, but the enormous stature of the skeletons and the fact that pine trees of centuries growth covered the spot go far to disprove this idea.

TORONTO, ONTARIO, DAILY TELEGRAPH, AUGUST 23, 1871
NIAGARA'S ANCIENT CEMETERY OF GIANTS
A REMARKABLE SIGHT: TWO HUNDRED SKELETONS IN CAYUGA TOWNSHIP

A SINGULAR DISCOVERY BY A TORONTONIAN AND OTHERS—A VAST GOLGOTHA OPENED TO VIEW—SOME REMAINS OF THE "GIANTS THAT WERE IN THOSE DAYS" FROM OUR OWN CORRESPONDENTS.

On Wednesday last, Rev. Nathaniel Wardell, Messers Orin Wardell (of Toronto), and Daniel Fredenburg were digging on the farm of the latter gentleman, which is on the banks of the Grand River, in the township of Cayuga.

When they got to five or six feet below the surface, a strange sight met them. Piled in layers, one upon top of the other, were some two hundred skeletons of human beings nearly perfect: around the neck of each one being a string of beads.

There were also deposited in this pit a number of axes and skimmers made of stone. In the jaws of several of the skeletons were large stone pipes, one of which Mr. O. Wardell took with him to Toronto a day or two after this Golgotha was unearthed.

These skeletons are those of men of gigantic stature, some of them measuring nine feet, very few of them being less than seven feet. Some of the thigh bones were found to be at least a foot longer than those at present known, and one of the skulls being examined completely covered the head of an ordinary person.

These skeletons are supposed to belong to those of a race of people anterior to the Indians.

Some three years ago, the bones of a mastodon were found embedded in the earth about six miles from this spot. The pit and its ghastly occupants are now open to the view of any who may wish to make a visit there.

RICHMOND, VIRGINIA, DAILY STATE JOURNAL,
SEPTEMBER 6, 1871
WONDERFUL DISCOVERIES
A Cave of Dead Indians

MAMMOTH REMAINS

We copy the following wonderful story from the Petersburg Index of this morning, and but for the reliable source from which it eminates, and the character of its informers, we would be disposed to doubt its truthfulness:

The following information is given us by gentlemen of the highest character and credit, who have seen with their own eyes, touched and tested with their own hands, the wonderful objects of which they make report:

The workmen engaged in opening a way for the projected railroad between Weldon and Garysburg, struck Monday, about one mile from the former place, in a bank beside the river, a catacomb of skeletons, supposed to be those of Indians of a remote age and a lost and forgotten race. The bodies exhumed were of a strange and remarkable formation. The skulls were nearly an inch in thickness: the teeth were filed sharp, as are those of cannibals, the enamel perfectly preserved; the bones were of wonderful length and strength — the femur being as long as the leg of an ordinary man, the stature of the body being probably as great as eight or nine feet. Near their heads were sharp stone arrows, stone mortars, in which their corn was brayed, and the bowls of pipes, apparently of soft, friable soapstone. The teeth of the skeletons are said to be as large as those of horses. One of them has been brought to the city, and presented to the officers of the Petersburg Railroad.

The bodies were found closely packed together, laid tier on tier, as it seemed. There was no discernible ingress or egress to the mound. The mystery is, who these giants were; to what race they belonged, to what era, and how they came to be buried there. To these inquiries no answer has yet been made; and meantime the ruthless spade continues to cleave body and skull asunder, throwing up in mingled masses the boner of the heroic tribe. We hope some effort will be made to preserve authentic and accurate accounts of these discoveries; and to throw some light, if possible, on the lost tribe, whose bones arc thus rudely disturbed from their sleep in earth's bosom.

[Note: This story was widely reprinted as a "new" story through the 1870s, but some details changed over time. The Petersburg Railroad appears as the Pittsburgh Railroad in 1874 reprints, for example.--)

HARTFORD, TENNESSEE WEEKLY TIMES, MARCH 30, 1872
RACE OF GIANTS FOUND IN UNDERGROUND TOMB UNDER "OLD STONE FORT" IN TENNESSEE

Near this city is a cave commonly known as "Bone Cave," from which have been brought, at various times, by boys and other persons who have tried to explore its hidden recesses, human bones of unusual size. The popular legends of the people are to the effect that it is somewhat connected with the people or race which created the "Old Stone Fort," which stands a short distance to the west of the town. A few days since some boys discovered an almost entire skeleton of mammoth size. The bones of the forearm were nearly twenty inches long, while the bone of the lower part of the leg was longer than an ordinary man's limb, foot and all. The jawbone of this giant would slip over the face of an ordinary man. Stimulated by these discoveries and a laudable desire to learn the secrets of this mysterious cavern, on last Thursday six gentlemen, including the editors of this paper, made this necessary preparation and started out to explore the "bone cave."

After an exhilarating walk of two miles through a clear bracing air, we reached the entrance of the cave, here divesting ourselves of our overcoats and lighting our torches, we entered one of the many passages, but after a short scramble we found further advance stopped by large pieces of rock that had fallen and blocked up the passage. Soon other members of the party came down and explorations commenced. We found ourselves in a vaulted chamber about twenty-five feet wide by sixty long, with passages leading in every direction. Following one, we rambled on for forty or fifty feet and then there appeared one of the most beautiful lakes we have ever seen. The water was clear and sweet and the ceiling over the water, studded with stalactites, reflected back the light from our torches like gems. We had no means of ascertaining the size of the lake, for the banks were perpendicular and it seemed like a pearl set in a bed of rocks. Another passage which was explored by B. F. Fleming was found to extend in a direct line toward the "Old Stone Fort."

This passage followed for a distance of nearly two hundred feet, when further progress was stopped by the passage being filled up with debris. This passage looks as if it had been cut from the solid rock by the and of man and gives rise to the hypothesis that at some time, far back in the dark ages, this cave a used by a race of men—giants if you like—that built this stone fort and the mounds and that this underground passage led from the fort to the cave, a mile distant. After a good look at this part of the cave, we returned to daylight, having been underground three hours and traversing over a mile inside the cave. After partaking of a lunch sent us by a very hospitable lady whose name we have mislaid—but not her kindness—we had a short search in the tunnel known as the "Dead House." Here we found many bones but all in a state of decomposition and decay. This tunnel or chamber is coated with a soft, loose soil to a depth of a foot or more, into which one can plunge a stick with perfect ease, while all the rest of the cave is solid rock.

EAU CLAIRE, WISCONSIN, DAILY FREE PRESS, OCTOBER 7, 1873
RAILROAD WORKERS UNEARTH GIANT
AN INDIAN MOUND OPENED

A few days ago the men engaged in building the road bed of the Green Bay and Winona railroad, struck an Indian mound near Arcadia. It had been in view for some days, and no little speculation was indulged in as to what the excavation would develop from this cemetery of the red man.

The discovery exceeded all anticipations. The skeleton of an Indian was found of such dimensions as to indicate that the frame must have been that of a giant. The jaw bone easily enclosed the face of the largest laborer to be found on the work. The thigh bones were more like those of a horse than a man, hair heavy and remarkably well-preserved.
Pieces of blanket in which the body had been wrapped were taken out in a tolerable state of preservation. A number of Mexican coins were also found.

The unusual size of the skeleton has excited considerable interest, and the curiosities will be carefully preserved for exhibition.

MONSTROUS!

Some interesting discoveries have just been made in a cave called, "King Solomon's Cave", Montana, United States, and an account of them is given by a correspondent of the Deer Lodge Independent who formed one of a party of explorers of the cave in question. After crawling through several narrow passages into a "most magnificent chamber", the attention of the explorers was attracted by a massive shield made of copper 57 inches in length and 36 inches in width leaning against the wall; about 10 feet beyond the shield, and eight feet from the floor, was a cavity in the wall. One of the party by the aid of some stones, climbed up to the aperture with a light but quickly descended in such a state of alarm that he was for some moments unable to explain that in the niche lay a petrified giant. The other explorers immediately climbed up to the aperture and gazed in. There, sure enough, was the monster man, whose dimensions on measurement were 9 feet 7 and a half inches, 38 inches across the breast and two feet deep. A helmet of brass or copper of gigantic proportions was on his head which, "the corrosive elements of time had sealed to his brow". He seems to have been a "disagreeable customer", and it is perhaps as well that he is dead and petrified, for near him were two mammoth spearheads, one of them with a socket of silver, into which to insert a large pole or handle. There was also a large hook made of bone, apparently manufactured from the tusk of a "leviathan of the land". On the wall were some strange looking letters and pictures of three ships, each having three masts, the middle mast being only two thirds the height of the outward ones. There was also on a flat stone in the wall the picture of a large man with a spear in his hand, and of another ship. On removing this stone, another chamber was discovered, in which were the bones of several more giants, a primitive quartz crusher, and a number of tools made of copper. It is supposed that these poor giants were at work a thousand years ago in the cave when a slide from the mountain above immured them in a living tomb. The search is to be further prosecuted; and in the meantime the explorers are described as "almost wild with the strange and curious things" they have discovered. This beats the "sea serpent" to fits.--Pall Mall Gazette.

NEW YORK TIMES, FEBRUARY 8, 1876
THE EARLY AMERICAN GIANT

The public will be unpleasantly reminded of the callous indifference to the future on the part of the prehistoric Americans by the recent discovery of three unusually fine skeletons in Kentucky. A Louisville paper asserts that two men lately undertook to explore a cave which they accidentally discovered not far from that city. The entrance to the cave was small, but the explorers soon found themselves in a magnificent apartment, richly furnished with the most expensive and fashionable stalactites. In a corner of this hall stood a large stone family vault, which the men promptly pried open. In it were found three skeletons, each nearly nine feet in height. The skeletons appear to have somewhat frightened the young men, for, on seeing so extensive collection of bones, they immediately dropped their torch, and subsequently wandered in darkness for thirty-six hours before they found their way back to daylight and soda-water.

Now, it is evident that these gigantic skeletons belonged to men very different from the men of present day. A skeleton eight feet and ten inches in height would measure fully nine feet when dressed in even a thin suit of flesh. The tallest nine-foot giant of a traveling circus is rarely more than six feet four inches high in private life and without his boots, and even giants of this quality are scarce and dear. The three genuine nine-foot men of Kentucky must have belonged to a race that is now entirely extinct, and hence it would be a matter of great interest if we could learn who and what they were.

MARION DAILY STAR, JULY 14, 1880
REMAINS OF NINE-FOOT GIANTS IN OHIO

A correspondent of the Cincinnati Enquirer, writing about the remains of a giant race found in Muskingum County, Ohio, says: The mound in which these remarkable discoveries were made was about sixty-four feet long and thirty-five feet wide top measurement and gently sloped down to the hill where it was situated. A number of stumps of trees were found on the slope standing in two rows, and on the top of the mound were an oak and a hickory stump, all of which bore marks of great age.

All of the skeletons were found on a level with the hill, and about eight feet from the top of the mound. In one grave there were two skeletons, one male and one female. The female face was looking downward, the male being immediately on top, with the face looking upward. The male skeleton measured nine feet in length, and the female was eight.

The male frame in this case was nine feet, four inches in length and the female was eight feet.

In another grave was found a female skeleton, which was encased in a clay coffin, holding in her arms the skeleton of a child three and a half feet long, by the side of which was an image, which being exposed to the atmosphere, crumbled rapidly.

The remaining seven, were found in single graves and were lying on their sides. The smallest of the seven was nine feet in length and the largest ten. One single circumstance connected with this discovery was the fact that not a single tooth was found in either mouth except in the one encased in the clay coffin.

On the south end of the mound was erected a stone altar, four and a half feet wide and twelve feet long, built on an earthen foundation nearly four feet wide, having in the middle two large flagstones, from which sacrifices were undoubtedly made, for upon them were found charred bones, cinders, and ashes. This was covered by about three feet of earth.

AN ANCIENT TABLET WITH POSSIBLE HIEROGLYPHS

What is now a profound mystery may in time became the key to unlock still further mysteries that were centuries ago commonplace affairs.

I refer to a stone that was found resting against the head of the clay coffin above described. It is irregularly shaped red sandstone, weighing about 18 pounds, being strongly impregnated with oxide of iron, and bearing upon one side TWO LINES OF HIEROGLYPHS.

SCIENTIFIC AMERICAN, AUGUST 14, 1880
ANCIENT AMERICAN GIANTS

The Rev. Stephen Bowers notes in the Kansas City Review of Science the opening of an interesting mound in Bush Creek Township, Ohio. The mound was opened by the Historical Society of the township, under the immediate supervision of Dr. J. E. Everhart of Zanesville.

It measured 65 by 34 feet at the summit, gradually sloping in every direction and was 8 feet in height.

There was found in it a sort of clay coffin including the skeleton of a woman measuring 8 feet in length. Within this coffin was found also a child about 3 and a half feet in length and an image that crumbled when exposed to the atmosphere.

In another grave was found the skeleton of a man and a woman, the former measuring nine and the latter 8 feet in length. In a third cave occurred two other skeletons, male and female, measuring respectively nine feet four inches and eight feet.

Seven other skeletons were found in the mound, thesmallest of which measured eight feet, while others eached the enormous length of ten feet. They wereburied singly or each in separate graves. Resting against one of the coffins was an engraved stone tablet (now in Cincinnati) from the characters on which Dr. Everhart and Mr. Bowers are led to conclude that this giant race were sun worshipers.

PROVIDENCE EVENING PRESS, SEPTEMBER 3,
1883
A GIANT'S SKELETON
MUST HAVE BEEN GOLIATH.

Hon J. H. Hainly, a well known and reliable citizen of Barnard, Mo., writes to the Gazette the particulars of the discovery of a giant skeleton four miles southwest of that place. A farmer named John W. Haunon found the bones protruding from the bank of a ravine that had been cut by the action of the rains during the past years. Mr. Hannon worked several days in unearthing the skeletons, which proved to be that of a human being whose height was twelve feet. The head through the temples was twelve inches; from the lower part of the skull at the back to the top was fifteen inches, and the circumference forty inches.
The ribs were nearly four feet long and one and three-quarter inches wide. The thigh bones were thirty inches long and large in proportion. When the earth was removed the ribs stood up high enough to enable a man to crawl in and explore the interior of the skeleton, turn around and come out with ease. The first joint of the great toe, above the nail, was

three inches long, and the entire foot eighteen inches in length. The skeleton lay on its face, twenty feet below the surface of the ground, and the toes embedded in the earth, indicating that the body either fell or was placed there when the ground was soft. The left arm was passed around backward, the head resting on the spinal column, while the right was stretched out to the front and right. Some of the bones crumbled upon exposure to the air, but many good specimens were preserved and are now on exhibition at Barnard. Medical men are much interested. The skeleton is generally pronounced a valuable relic of the prehistoric race.

[NOTE: This article previously appeared in the Galveston Gazette on August 15.--

----

HELENA INDEPENDENT, OCTOBER 10, 1883
PREHISTORIC GIANT SKELETON FOUND

J. H. Hamley, a well known and reliable citizen of Barnard, Mo., writes to the Gazette, the particulars of the discovery of a GIANT skeleton, four miles southwest of that place.

A farmer named John W. Hannon, found the bones protruding from the bank of a ravine that has been cut by the action of the rains during the past years.

Mr. Hannon worked several days in unearthing "the skeleton," which proved to be that of a human being whose height was twelve feet.

The head through the temples was eleven inches; from the lower part of the skull at the back to the top was fifteen inches, and the circumference forty inches. The ribs were nearly four feet long, one and three-fourths inches wide. The thigh bones we're thirty-six inches long and large in proportion.

When the earth was removed the ribs stood high enough to enable a man to crawl in and explore the interior of the skeleton, turn around and come out with ease.

The first joint of the greater toe above the nail, was three inchen long, and the entire foot, eighteen inches in length. The skeleton lay on its face twenty feet below the surface of the ground and the toes were imbedded in the earth, indicating that the body either fell or was placed there when the ground was soft.
The left arm was passed around backward, the hand resting on the spinal column, while the right arm was stretched out to the front, and right. Some of the bones crumbled on exposure to the air, but many good specimens were preserved, and are now exhibited at, Bernard Medical school.
The skeleton is generally pronounced a relic of the prehistoric race.

ATHENS, GEORGIA, BANNER, MAY 6, 1884
GIANT CROWNED ROYALTY IS FOUND

Athens, Georgia: Mr. J. B. Toomer yesterday received a letter from Mr. Hazelton, who is on a visit to Cartersville. The letter contained several beads made of stone, and gave an interesting account of the opening of a large Indian mound near that town by a committee of scientists sent out from the Smithsonian Institution. After removing the dirt for some distance, a layer of large flag stones was found, which had evidently been dressed by hand, and showed that the men who quarried this rock understood their business.

The stones were removed, when in a kind of vault beneath them, the skeleton of a giant, who measured seven feet two inches, was found.

His hair was coarse and jet black and hung to his waist, the brow being ornamented with a copper crown. The skeleton was remarkably well-preserved and taken from the vault intact. Near this skeleton were found the bodies of several small children of various sizes. The remains of the latter were covered with beads, made of bone of some kind. Upon removing these, the bodies were found to be encased in a network made of straw or reed, and beneath this was the covering of an animal of some kind.

In fact, the bodies had been prepared somewhat after the manner of mummies, and will doubtless throw new light on the history of the people who raised the mounds.

Upon the stones that covered the vault were carved inscriptions, which, if deciphered, will probably lift the veil that has enshrouded the history of the race of giants that undoubtedly at one time inhabited the continent.

ALL THE RELICS WERE SHIPPED TO THE SMITHSONIAN

All the relics were carefully packed and sent to the Smithsonian Institution, and are said to be the most interesting collection ever found in America.

The explorers are now at work on a mound in Barlow County, and before their return home will visit various sections of Georgia where antiquities are found. On the Oconee River, in Greene County, just above Powell's Mills, are several mounds, one of them very tall and precipitous.

[NOTE: This article previously appeared in the Washington Post on March 16.--.]

NEW YORK TIMES, MAY 5, 1885
SKELETONS SEVEN FEET LONG

Centerburg, Ohio: Licking County has been for years a favorite field for students of Indian history. Last week a small mound near Homer was opened by some school boys. Today further search was made and several feet below the surface of the earth, in a large vault with stone floor and bark covering, were found four huge skeletons, three being over seven feet in length, and the other a full eight feet.

The skeletons lay with their feet to the east on a bed of charcoal in which were numerous burned bones. About the neck of the largest skeleton were a lot of stone beads. The grave contained about 30 stone vessels and implements, the most striking being a curiously-wrought pipe. It is said to be the only engraved stone pipe ever found. A stone kettle, holding about a gallon in which was a residue of saline matter, bears evidence of much skill. Their bows, a number of arrows, stone hatchets, and a stone knife are among the implements that were found at the site.

PHILADELPHIA TIMES, JUNE 27, 1885
GIANTS FOUND ON THE NEW YORK-
PENNSYLVANIA STATE LINE

"Why this man was ten or twelve feet high."

"Thunder and lightning!" exclaimed Mr. Porter in astonishment. The first speaker, who has won local distinction as a scientist, reiterated his assertion.

J. H. Porter has a farm near Northeast, not many miles from where the Lake Shore Railroad crosses the New York state boundary line. Early this week some workmen in Mr. Porter's employ came upon the entrance to a cave and on entering it found heaps of human bones within. Many skeletons were complete and specimens of the find were brought out and exhibited to the naturalists and archaeologists of the neighborhood. They informed the wondering bystanders that the remains were unmistakably those of giants.

The entire village of Northeast was aroused by the discovery and today hundreds of people from this city took advantage of their holiday to visit the scene. It was first conjectured that the remains were those of soldiers killed in battle with the Indians that abounded in the vicinity during the last century, but the size of the skulls and the length of the leg bones dispelled that theory. So far about 150 giant skeletons of powerful proportions have been exhumed and indications point to a second cave eastward, which may probably contain as many more. Scientists who have exhumed skeletons and made careful measurements of the bones say that they are the remains of a race of gigantic creatures, compared with which our tallest men would appear pygmies. There are no arrow-heads, stone hatchets, or other implements of war with the bodies. Some of the bones are on exhibition at the various stores. One is as thick as a good sized bucket.

THE NEW YORK TIMES, APRIL 5, 1886
MONSTER SKULLS AND BONES

CARTERSVILLE, Ga., April 4.—The water has receded from the Tumlin Mound Field, and has left uncovered acres of skulls and bones. Some of these are gigantic. If the whole frame is in proportion to two thigh bones that were found, the owners must have stood 14 feet high. Many curious ornaments of shell, brass, and stone have been found. Some of the bodies were buried in small vaults built of stones. The whole makes a mine of archæological wealth. A representative of the Smithsonian Institution is here investigating the curious relics.

STEVENS POINT DAILY JOURNAL, MAY 1, 1886
OHIO ACCOUNT OF NINE-FOOT GIANTS

It is very evident that at an early day in the history of this country, this section of Ohio was an important camping ground for the American Indian. And, indeed, discoveries are frequently made, which lead people interested in the matter of prehistoric America to believe that a race of mankind, superior in size, strength, and intelligence to the common red man of the forest, flourished not only along the coasts East and South, but right here in southern Ohio. There are in this county several burying grounds, and two of them are located five miles west of this city, near Jasper, one on the farm of Mr. William Bush and one on Mr. Matthew Mark's farm. In a conversation with a gentleman who has seen [skeletons] unearthed at the Mark bank, we were told that many dozens of human skeletons have been exhumed since the bank was first opened.

Some of these skeletons have been measured, and the largest have been found to be nine feet long and over.

At one time ten skeletons were exhumed. They had been buried in a circle, standing in an erect position, and were in a comparatively well-preserved condition. One remarkable fact about all the skeletons unearthed at these places is the perfect state of preservation in which their teeth are found to be.

Not a decayed tooth has been discovered, and this would seem to indicate that these people naturally had excellent teeth or some extraordinary manner of preserving them.

OSHKOSH, WISCONSIN, DAILY NORTHWESTERN, JULY 8, 1886 GIANT SKELETON FOUND IN PETERSBURG, KENTUCKY

At Petersburg, Kentucky, twenty-five miles below here, an excavation for a new building has brought to light a peculiar find; it being a strange-looking Indian grave, the receptacle of which has been made of stone and clay, formed into a kind of cement, about three feet in height, and fully nine feet in length.

Within the rude vault lay a giant human skeleton that measured seven feet, two inches, in length. The bones were all of large proportions, and the monstrous skull, with teeth perfect and intact, was more than half an inch thick at the base.

A number of copper pieces, evidently worn for ornaments, a stone pipe, and a quantity of arrowheads were found with the decaying bones.

ASHBURTON GUARDIA, NOVEMBER 1887, ALLEGED DISCOVER OF THE BODY OF A GIANT

The oil city (Penn) "Simety" is responsible for the following: While William Thompson, assisted by Robert R. Smith, was engaged in making an excavation near the house of the former, about a half mile north of West Hickory, preparatory to erecting a derrick, they exhumed an enormous helmet of iron which was corroded with rust. Further digging brought to a light sword, which measured 9 feet in length. Curiosity incited them to enlarge the hole, and after a little time they discovered the bones of two enormous feet. Following up the "lead" they had so unexpectedly struck, in few hours time they had unearthed a well-preserved skeleton of an enormous giant, belong to a species of the human family which probably inhabited this and other parts of the world at the time of which the Bible speaks, when it says, "and there were giants in those days". The helmet is said to be in the shape of those found among the ruins of Nineveh. The bones of the skeleton are remarkably white. The teeth are all in their places and all of them are double and of extraordinary size. These relics have been taken to Tionesta, where they are visited by large numbers of people daily. When his giantship was in the flesh, he must have stood 18 feet in his stockings. These remarkable relics will be forwarded to New York early next week. The joints of the skeleton are now being glued together. These remains were found 12 feet below the surface of a mound which had been thrown up probably centuries ago and which was not more than 3 feet above the level of the ground around it. Here is another nut for antiquarians to crack.

CINCINNATI COMMERCIAL, OCTOBER 7, 1888
INDIANA GIANTS FOUND
BONES OF AN INDIAN GIANT

A member of the Logan Grays, the crack military organization of Logansport that held its encampment this year at Eagle Lake, near Warsaw stopped in this city on his way home from camp and told the following story of the discovery by the party of a cavern on an island in Eagle Lake; A.M. Jones rowed to a small island near the southwest corner of the lake and began digging for worms.

He turned over a large, flat stone near a tree, and under it was a small hole, which was an entrance to a cave. Jones called the boys up, and we began an exploration of the cavern, which proved to be twenty-five feet long, fifteen feet wide, and eight feet deep. The walls are of a natural formation of stone, branching out at the middle so as to form two rooms.

In the front room was the skeleton of a man six feet

nine inches long. The bones were very large, indicating great strength. Along one side of the cave runs a small stream of water, as pure as crystal. In the front of it forms a small pool. In this were a number of bones. Old settlers in this vicinity of the lake claim that the skeleton is that of Eagleonkie, the giant Indian chief who lived alone on this island and mysteriously disappeared during a severe winter. The island was known after this chief and was once known as Giant Island.

MERIDEN, CONNECTICUT DAILY REPUBLICAN, JULY 8, 1889
A PREHISTORIC BASEBALL BAT
GIGANTIC SKELETONS AND OTHER WONDERS DISCOVERED BY AN EXCITED FANCY

St. Paul, July 8.--Every resident of Montana and many visitors to the famous territory know that the Belt Mountains have always been the seat of mysterious stories, and that in their numerous gulches and canyons have been picked up wonderful relics. Among the most curious are agatized human maxillaries and teeth, all of gigantic size. Gold in quantities has been found in the Belt Mountains and rubies, sapphires, and even diamonds are shown as product of one or the other portions of the territory. The Helena correspondent of the Pioneer–Press sends a remarkable story, accompanied by numerous attestations to its truth. A gold hunter said that while prospecting in the Belt Mountains he found a peculiar depression in the ground. After excavating he discovered a mysterious cavern, reached by twenty-three steps. "At the foot of the stairs," said he, "on one side of the passage lay the skeleton of a man of immense stature. The skeleton measured exactly nine feet six inches in height. The skull lay a few inches from the trunk, and between the two lay 27 nuggets. They were strung on a fine gold wire, and ranged from one ounce to ten in weight. Around the thigh, arm, and shin bones were other strings of nuggets, none of which weighed more than 4 ounces. There were about 15 pieces of gold in the pile. They were of many different shapes. None of them weighed over 3 ounces, and each piece had a hole through the center. On each side of the skull I found some sort of precious stones. They lay in a tiny golden basket, and were evidently worn in the ears. I do not know what name to give them, but I believe they are rubies."

"Beside the trunk of the skeleton, I found a copper axe, with an edge harder and keener than any steel instrument of the kind I have ever seen. On the opposite side was a club made of the same metal as the axe. It was shaped not unlike a baseball bat. Under the trunk was a gold plate ten inches long, six inches wide, and one-eighth of an inch thick. It was covered with strange devices. A little further on lay another skeleton, that of a woman. I picked up a string of nuggets near this skull also. They were perfectly round and exactly the same size. They weighed about 3 ounces apiece. Every now and then I came to other skeletons, and, although by nearly every one of them I found necklaces, yet strange to say they were of round copper balls."

"The catacombs as I have named this passage, are about 300 feet long, fourteen feet wide, and thirty high, and seem to have been cut out of the solid rock. At the end of the gallery is a room sixty feet square and forty high. In the center of this room stands a block of granite about twelve feet square and four feet high. It seems as though the rock had been hewn out around it. It is perfectly square, and it is exactly the same distance from the walls of the room on every side. There are steps cut in the rock leading to the top of the hall. On the top stands another block of granite, ten feet long, four wide, and three high. This is hollowed out in the shape of a human form. I lay down in this and, though I am not a small man by any means, yet the mold was much too large for me. Around the room were scattered vessels of clay, some of which will hold 25 gallons. They are light, yet tougher than wrought iron. I tried to break one of them by dashing it against the granite flooring of the room. I could not even scratch it. Altogether I gathered up 500 ounces of gold in the underground passage."

CUBA, NEW YORK, CUBA PATRIOT, OCTOBER 10, 1889
OHIO MOUND RELICS
GIGANTIC MAN BURIED ALONGSIDE A COLOSSAL PANTHER

Soon after the 1st of March I left for Southern Ohio to collect relics to be placed on loan exhibition in the Smithsonian Institution at Washington. During the last two months eleven mounds have been opened and their contents taken to the museum and placed on exhibition.

These mounds vary in height from eight to thirty feet, are generally conical in shape, and contain all the way from 300 to 10,000 square yards of dirt. They were built by the aborigines of this country hundreds of years ago to serve as burial places for the distinguished dead. They are generally placed near some stream in a valley and not infrequently on high points of land, which command a good view of the country, but the larger ones are in the valleys. These mounds are usually composed of clay, sometimes of sand, and often have layers of charcoal or burnt clay in them. These layers are often as brightly colored as if they had been painted. [...]

About five feet above this layer, or nine feet from the summit of the mound, was a skeleton of a very large individual who had buried by the side of it the bones of a panther. Whether the person had killed the panther and it was buried with him as an honor, or whether the panther had killed the individual, I cannot say. This much, however, can be said, that in 43 mounds opened no find of this nature has been made. It is therefore quite interesting and important. The skull of this panther was very large, teeth very long and sharp. It would take a mound builder of a great deal of nerve to attack a beast of this size if he had nothing but a stone hatchet and bow and arrows to defend himself with. Just below this skeleton and lying on the layer of buried bones was a medium-sized personage who had buried around his neck in the manner of a necklace, between his upper and lower jaw, 147 bone and shell beads. The shell beads were made from the thick part of Conch and Pyrula shells. These shells must have been carried from the Atlantic Ocean, as they are ocean shells, and not found inland, or the tribe to which the man belonged may have traded with tribes near the ocean and thereby got the beads. [...]--Cincinnati Courier Gazette [September 26, 1889].

THE POPULAR SCIENCE NEWS, AUGUST 1890
A PRE-HISTORIC GIANT.

The legends of all races tell of a time when mankind were of giant stature, doubtless arising, in many cases, from the discovery of the fossil bones of ancient animals of large size, such as the elephant, mammoth, etc. But, as far as we know, there is no proof whatever that the human race was ever possessed of a greater average stature than at present. In fact, the tendency seems to be in the opposite direction, the men of the present time slightly exceeding their ancestors in size—a result doubtless due to the improved conditions of existence in these latter days.

Occasional instances of unusual stature are, however, not uncommon, and can be seen in almost any dime museum; and that there were giants even in the Stone Age seems to be proved by a discovery made near Montpellier, in France, by M. LAPOUGE, and communicated by him to La Nature. At Castelnau, near the above town, is a prehistoric cemetery, dating from the ages of polished stone and bronze. A large number of human bones were found, including about forty skulls, one of which formerly belonged to an individual about eighteen years old, who, judging from the size of his skull, must have been over six feet in height.

But the most remarkable "finds" of M. Lapouge were three pieces of bone, illustrated in the engraving, which must formerly have belonged to some pre-historic giant of extraordinary size. The first piece, shown on the left of the engraving, is a part of a femur, or thigh-bone, and the one on the right a part of a tibia, or shin-bone. In the middle is represented a humerus, or bone of the upper arm, from the same ancient cemetery, but of normal size. At the bottom is represented a small fragment, which may be either a piece of a femur or a humerus; if the latter, then it must also have formerly made up part of the skeleton of the giant, as can be seen by comparison with the normal humerus above it.

If we judge of the height of this neolithic giant by the usual proportion of the parts of the skeleton to each other, he must have been between ten and eleven feet high. The question remains whether this excessive growth was a normal one, or due to a diseased condition resulting in a general hypertrophy of the osseous system. On this point the authorities differ, one professor of the University of Montpellier holding that the bones are normal in every respect, while another finds evidence of a diseased condition. In either case the giant of Castelnau must have been a source of wonder, if not of terror, to the savage men of those times, and was doubtless treated with all the honor which in these modern days is bestowed upon a successful prize-fighter.

There has been an old tradition among the peasants of the vicinity that a cavern in the valley was, in olden times, occupied by a giant; and it would be curious if the discovery of M. Lapouge should show it to be founded on fact, and handed down from father to son during the centuries that have elapsed since the time when the ancient inhabitants of France knew of no other material for their implements and utensils than the stones which they so laboriously worked into the desired shapes.

THE NEW YORK TIMES, JULY 5, 1891
MR. JEFFERSON'S CYCLOPS.
A GIANT SKELETON UNEARTHED AT
BUZZARD'S BAY

BUZZARD'S BAY, Mass., July 4.—Joseph Jefferson, the actor, has made an astonishing find on the Summer place which he has purchased here near that of ex-President Cleveland. In laying out the grounds and making alterations it became necessary to remove a sandhill of large size. The workmen, while doing this, found the skeleton of a man that filled them with astonishment from its great size.

When an attempt was made to lift up the skeleton it crumbled away, all except the skull. A workman lay down by the side of it, however, and it was estimated that it must have belonged to a man at least 6 feet 5 or 6 inches in height. The most peculiar thing was brought to light, however, when the skull was taken to Mr. Jefferson and by him examined. It was like ordinary skulls, only larger, except that it had so far as could be seen, no place where the eyes had been.

There was one hole in the center of the forehead that might have once served for one eye. This led Mr. Jefferson to believe that he had, perhaps, discovered the skeleton of a Cyclops.

He said to Mr. Booth, who was paying him a visit, when he saw the wonderful skull, that he and his brother actor had a chance at hand to play "Hamlet" with a skull such as it had never been played with before. All the scientific gentlemen in the neighborhood have been unable to give an explanation of the skull as were Mr. Jefferson and Mr. Booth. Mr. Jefferson will no doubt be grateful to receive suggestions from men of science that may throw light on the matter.

ST. PAUL DAILY GLOBE, FEBRUARY 24, 1891
PETRIFIED GIANT
DISCOVERY OF A BODY WITH LEGS EIGHT FEET IN LENGTH

HELENA, MT, Feb 23 – Vital Jarcot, a half-breed, who carries mail between Ft. McGinnis and Rocky Point, brings the news of a discovery of the petrified remains of a giant in the badlands of Choteau county, a few miles below the mouth of the Mussel Shell River. The discovery was made by Lata Dona, another half-breed, who started off to find a purchaser for his curiosity before Jarcot could get a complete description. The remains were not complete, showing the petrifaction had only taken place in a portion of the body, while the remainder had followed the course of nature and returned to dust. One leg was 8 feet long, the thigh being about 4 feet. A rib found measured 2½ feet. Petrifaction is no unusual thing in the badlands of Montana and the Dakotas. Wood in that state is frequently found. The petrified body of an Indian was found in North Dakota about a year ago. Jarcot, who brings the story was perfectly sober.

NEW YORK SUN, AUGUST 27, 1891
GIANT SKELETON FOUND IN UTAH

The gigantic skeleton of a man, measuring 8 feet 6 inches in height, was found near the Jordan River just outside Salt Lake City, last week. The find was made by a workman who was digging an irrigation ditch. The skull was uncovered at a depth of eight feet from the surface of the ground and the skeleton was standing bolt upright. The workmen had to dig down nine feet in order to exhume it. The bones were much decayed and crumbled at the slightest touch. They were put together with great care and the skeleton was found to measure 8 feet 6 inches in height: the skull measured 11 inches in diameter and the feet 19 inches long. A copper chain, to which was attached three medallions covered with curious hieroglyphics, was found around the neck of the skeleton and near it were found a stone hammer, some pieces of pottery, an arrowhead, and some copper medals. Archaeologists believe that the original owner of the skeleton belonged to the race of mound builders.

BURLINGTON, IOWA, HAWK EYE, SEPTEMBER 1, 1891
PERFECT GIANT SKELETON FOUND

No little excitement has been occasioned by the discovery on a farm near Carthage of several skeletons in a mound that are doubtless those of prehistoric people. In regard to this historic find the Carthage Republican newspaper will publish the following.

The Sweney Farm Mounds, located near the south line of the farm quarter, on Section Five, Carthage Township, have been a familiar landmark to the oldest citizens since, and the quarter was entered by Samuels in 1836, or thereabouts.

Last Saturday afternoon the new owner of the Sweney Farm Indian Mounds was plowing on one of his mounds when he hit a series of sandstone blocks. On the removal of several sandstone rocks embedded in the ground, the owner Mr. Felt procured a spade and proceeded to dig out the rocks with some difficulty.

On the removal of these rocks there was revealed an almost perfect skeleton of a man of very large size. The authorities of Carthage College have secured permission to investigate the find to its fullest extent and Rev. Dr. Stephen D. Peet has been notified.

CENTRALIA, OHIO, ENTERPRISE, NOVEMBER 21, 1891
WORLD'S FAIR DIG LEADS TO GIANT MONARCH
GIGANTIC SKELETON, EVIDENTLY OF A PREHISTORIC MONARCH, EXHUMED IN OHIO

Chillicothe, Ohio: Warren K. Morehead and Dr. Cresson, who have been prosecuting excavations here for the past two months in the interest of the World's Fair, have just made one of the richest finds of the century in the way of prehistoric remains.

Those gentlemen have confined their excavation to the Hopewell Farm, seven miles from here, upon which are located some twenty-odd Indian mounds. On Saturday, they were at work on a mound 500 feet long, 200 feet wide and 28 feet high. At the depth of 14 feet, near the center of the mound, they exhumed the massive skeleton of a man encased in copper armor. The head was covered in an oval-shaped copper cap, the jaws had copper mouldings, the arms were dressed in copper, while copper plates covered the chest and stomach and on each side of the head, on protruding sticks were wooden antlers ornamented with copper.

The mouth was stuffed with genuine pearls of immense size, but much decayed. Around the neck was a necklace of bear's teeth set with pearls.

At the side of the male skeleton was also found a female skeleton, the two being supposed to be man and wife. Mr. Morehead and Mr. Cresson believe they have at last found the "King of the Mound Builders."

ARIZONA REPUBLICAN, FEBRUARY 27, 1892
THERE WERE GIANTS IN THOSE DAYS

Wheeling, W. Va., – While digging a grave on Trace Fork, Lincoln county, a few days ago, the bones of a human being of gigantic stature and proportions were exhumed. The skeleton is in a good state of preservation and the outlines of the frame sufficiently defined to determine that the stature of the person must have been nine or ten feet. The skull and other bones also indicate prodigious size. No one now living has any knowledge of the grave or its occupant, and all indications point to its belonging to some prehistoric race of giants contemporary with Mastodons, fossil remains of which have been found in many parts of the country.

CHICAGO TRIBUNE, 1892 [date unknown]
HUNDREDS OF BURIALS

Near Carthage, Illinois, about one year ago, a mound was plowed up and the bones, principally the skulls of human beings, were found in sufficient quantities to warrant the conclusion that hundreds of people had been buried there. From measurements taken of some of the skulls and principal bones, it was decided that the persons buried were of a race of giants. Some of the femur bones measured 19¼ inches, and the measurements of the skulls and other bones indicated that these people must have attained an average of seven to eight feet in height.

THE PITTSBURGH DISPATCH, AUGUST 23, 1892
TWO GIANT HUMAN SKELETONS FOUND.

BEAVER FALLS, Aug. 22.—[Special]—Workmen, while digging a ditch from the new shovel works to the river at Allquippa to-day, unearthed the remains of two skeletons. They are of gigantic size, and are supposed to be the remains of two Indians. They have been in the ground for many years, as the larger bones and skull only remain.

THE SUN, DECEMBER 8, 1893
9 FOOT MUMMY DISCOVERED IN
PENNSYLVANIA BURIAL MOUND

Dr W. J. Holland, curator of the Carnegie museum, Pittsburg and his assistant, Dr. Peterson, a few days ago opened up a mound of the ancient race that inhabited this section and secured the skeleton of a man who when in the flesh was between eight and nine feet in height, says a Greensburg (Pa.) dispatch to the Philadelphia Inquirer.

This mound which was originally about 100 feet longer and more than 12 feet high has been somewhat worn down by time. It is on the J. R. Secrist farm in South Huntington township. This farm has been in the Secrist name for more than a century.

The most interesting feature in the recent excavation was the mummified torso of the human body, which the experts figured was laid to rest at least 400 years ago. Portions of the bones dug up and the bones in the legs, Prof, Peterson declares are those of a person between eight and nine feet in height. The scientists figure that that this skeleton was the framework of a person of the prehistoric race that inhabited this section before the American Indians.

The torso and the portions of the big skeleton were shipped to the Carnegie museum. Drs. Holland and Peterson supervised the exploration on the Secrist mound with the greatest of care. The curators believe the man whose skeleton they secured belonged to the mound builders class.

THE NEW YORK TIMES, MARCH 5, 1894
GIANTS OF OTHER DAYS.

Recent Discoveries near Serpent Mound, Ohio

From the Indianapolis Journal.

Farmer Warren Cowen of Hilsborough, Ohio, while fox hunting recently discovered several ancient graves. They were situated upon a high point of land in Highland County, Ohio, about a mile from the famous Serpent Mound, where Prof. Putnam of Harvard made interesting discoveries. As soon as the weather permitted, Cowen excavated several of these graves. The graves were made of large limestone slabs, two and a half to three feet in length and a foot wide. These were set on edge about a foot apart. Similar slabs covered the graves. A single one somewhat larger was at the head and another at the foot. The top of the grave was two feet below the present surface.

Upon opening one of the graves a skeleton of upwards of six feet was brought to light. There were a number of stone hatchets, beads, and ornaments of peculiar workmanship near the right arm. Several large flint spear and arrow heads among the ribs gave evidence that the warrior had died in battle.

In another grave was the skeleton of a man equally large. The right leg had been broken during life, and the bones had grown together. The protuberance at the point of union was as large as an egg, and the limb was bent like a bow. At the feet lay the skull of some enemy or slave. Several pipes and pendants were near the shoulders.

In other graves, Cowen made equally interesting finds. It seems that the region was populated by a fairly intelligent people, and that the serpent mound was an object of worship. Near the graves is a large field in which broken implements, fragments of pottery, and burned stones give evidence of a prehistoric village.

THE WORLD, OCTOBER 7, 1895
BIGGEST GIANT EVER KNOWN

Nine Feet High and Probably a California Indian

Measurement Well Authentiated

Other Big Men and Women of Fact and Fable Who Are Famous Types if Giantism

The corpse of the biggest man that ever lived has been dug up near San Diego California. At all events there is no satisfactory read in ancient or modern history of any human being nearly so tall. The mummy--for in such a condition the remains were found--is that of a person would have been about nine feet high in life. This makes allowances for the shrinkage, which may be pretty closely calculated.

As to the accuracy in the estimate there can no question, as the cadaver has been carefully inspected and measured by Prof. Thomas Wilson, Curator of the Department of Prehistoric Anthropology in the Smithsonian Institution, and by other scientists. The tapeline even now registers the length from heel to top of the head at eight feet four inches.

The mummy is that of an Indian and is almost certainly prehistoric, though its age cannot be determined with any sort of accuracy. Historical records of the part of California where it was found go back for at least 250 years, and they make no mention of any man of gigantic stature. How much older the body may be must be left open to conjecture. Its preservation, its preservation is no matter of surprise, in that arid region the atmospheric conditions are such that a corpse buried in the dry season might very well become perfectly desiccated before the arrival of the rains, and thus be rendered permanently proof against decay.

The body was found in a cave by a party of prospectors. Over the head are the remnants of a leather hood. The man was well advanced in years.

It has been stated that the man must have surpassed in height any giant of whom there is an historical record. This is unquestionably true so far as the last two centuries are concerned, and accounts of older dates are not well authenticated. Indeed they grow more and more apocryphal as distant in time increases. [...]

MAYSVILLE, KENTUCKY PUBLIC LEDGER, MAY 31, 1897
GIANT SKELETONS FOUND

CHILLECOTHE, O., May 31. – Ten skeletons were found in two mounds by Dr. Loveberry, curator of the Ohio State University Museum, one that of a giant fully eight feet tall. It is the most notable find yet.

SYRACUSE DAILY STANDARD, JULY 23, 1897
HUNDREDS OF MOUNDS, EMBALMED NINE-FOOT GIANT, AND DAMS

While men were excavating with a steam shovel near Mora, Minnesota, they found an old copper spear with a point measuring 10 inches in length and tapering to a very fine and tempered point. The weapon shows the maker to have been an adept in working copper metal. Archaeologists believe that at some prehistoric time the country surrounding Mora was densely inhabited by a race of people who were much further advanced in civilization than the Indians.

 The many mounds around Fish Lake show that a mighty race of people lies slumbering there, whose history is as yet unwritten—from the mounds of earth, which were used as sepultures for their dead, and which demonstrate beyond a doubt that they were a numerous as well as powerful people.

BALTIMORE AMERICAN, NOVEMBER 15, 1897
BONES OF GIANT INDIANS FOUND IN
MARYLAND
PREHISTORIC MEN SEVEN FEET TALL WHO
ONCE LIVED IN WHAT IS MARYLAND

There has just been received at the Maryland Academy of Sciences, the skeleton of an Indian seven feet tall. It was discovered near Antietam. There are now skeletons of three powerful Indians at the Academy who at one time in their wildness roamed over the state of Maryland armed with such instruments as nature gave them or that their limited skill taught them to make.

Two of these skeletons belonged to individuals evidently of gigantic size. The vertebrae and bones of the legs are nearly as thick as those of a horse and the length of the long bones exceptional.

The skulls are of fine proportions, ample and with walls of moderate thickness and of great strength and stiffened beyond with a powerful occipital ridge. The curves of the forehead are moderate and not retreating, suggesting intelligence and connected with jaws of moderate development. The locality from which these skeletons came is in Frederick County, near Antietam Creek. It was formerly supposed to have been the battleground of two tribes of Indians: the Catawbas and the Delawares.

Before the coming of the white man, this site was occupied as a village by Indians of great stature, some of them six-and-a-half to seven feet in height.

THE NEW YORK TIMES, DECEMBER 20, 1897
WISCONSIN MOUND OPENED
Skeleton Found of a Man Over Nine Feet High with an Enormous Skull.

MAPLE CREEK, Wis., Dec. 19.—One of the three recently discovered mounds in this town has been opened. In it was found the skeleton of a man of gigantic size. The bones measured from head to foot over nine feet and were in a fair state of preservation. The skull was as large as a half bushel measure. Some finely tempered rods of copper and other relics were lying near the bones.
The mound from which these relics were taken is ten feet height and thirty feet long, and varies from six to eight feet in width. The two mounds of lesser size will be excavated soon.

OHIO SCIENCE ANNUAL, 1898
GIANT EIGHT FEET, SEVEN INCHES TALL
UNEARTHED

A rare archaeological discovery has been made near Reinersville in Morgan County, Ohio. A small knoll, which had always been supposed to be the result of an uprooted tree, was opened recently and discovered to be the work of mound builders.

Just below the surrounding surface, a layer of boulders and pebbles was found. Directly underneath this was found the skeleton of a giant 8 feet, 7 inches in height. Surrounding the skeleton were bone and stone implements, stone hatchets, and other characteristics of the mound builders.

The discovery is considered by the scientists as one of the most important ever made in Ohio. The skeleton is now in the possession of a Reinersville collector.

KEWANNA HERALD, AUGUST 18, 1898
PLOWED UP AN INDIAN

For two centuries, at least, the body has lain crumbling away to mother earth. Who can speak the weal and woe, the heart ache and joy thus represented? It is like a breeze from another world, and life seems fleeting faster still as one gazes on the remains of a once glorious union, now silent evermore.

SKELETON INDIAN BRAVE FOUND NEAR SHADY DELL

The finding of arrowheads and stone axes that were used by the roaming Indians of other days is a common enough occurrence, but this week there was disinterred the bones of one of these ancient inhabitants, which has made it the talk of the community. Charley Dukes, on the old family farm near Shady Dell School House, while plowing near a large, old oak stump, the tree of which was cut down over forty years ago, turned up the skeleton of a giant of the Indian occupation of this country.

For years, two large rocks in the field, which had the appearance of being perfectly placed, have been the wonder of the Dukes family, but now they find that the mound in which the bones were found is directly on the line between these stones, designating, therefore, the place of burial like our tombstones of today. The bones are those of a large person, although the two centuries of summer and winter have dealt severely with them. The remains show parts of the femur, tibia, innominate, phalanges, and several face bones including some very well-preserved teeth.

MANY SKELETON OF AN EXTINCT INDIAN RACE UNEARTHED IN THE HOOSIER STATE

A huge gravel pit has been opened at Whitlock, Indiana. Soon after the excavating began a skeleton was found and as the pit widened other skeletons were unearthed until at least thirty graves had been opened and many skeletons brought to light, evidently the remains of an Indian tribe.

One skeleton was found beneath a large stump, and another was found twelve feet underground. The graves appear in regular order, and the occupants were buried in a sitting posture. In one grave three skeletons, supposed to be those of a woman and two children, were found.

The other day the largest specimen was unearthed, the body of a person who in life must have been a giant.

A peculiarity of the skeletons is that the teeth are nearly all in a perfect state of preservation. In one grave beside the human skeletons was that of a dog, a copper spearhead, an earthen pot, and numerous beads proving that some important personage had been put to rest there.

FOND DU LAC BANNER, JUNE 6, 1899
GIANT INDIAN BONES: DISCOVERY OF AN
EXTRA ORDINARY SKELETON NEAR
FOND DU LAC

An Indian skeleton was dug up on the farm of Matt and Joseph Leon, one mile south of St. Cloud on Saturday. There is nothing strange in finding an Indian skeleton, but this one was a giant in size, his frame measuring seven feet. He must have been a man of note among his people, for he was buried in a large mound, sixteen handsome arrows surrounding his body. The skull was brought to this city and is on exhibition in one of the Main Street windows.

YOUNGSTON VINDICATOR, AUGUST 5, 1899
NEW RACE OF GIANTS
MONSTERS OF HUMANITY IN THE SOUTH
POLAR REGIONS

Some papers are exploiting photographs of a race of giants said to have been discovered by Fredrick A. Cook, who has just returned from an exploring expedition to the south Polar Regions. The existence of such a race has always been denied by scientists, but Dr. Cook, it is said, has not only seen and talked with them, but brings back photographs to prove beyond argument that the biggest race of human beings in the world is to found in the frozen south.

The monstrous forms of both the men and women are clad in furs. The men arm themselves with bows and arrows and wooden clubs. Their strength and endurance are remarkable. The men can outrun any horse on a long stretch. They can cover 50 miles in a few hours. To see a company of these wild men crossing a plain is like watching a herd of antelope skim over the ground. Only their upright position, with their scanty goats' skins flying in the wind and the flourish of their clubs and bows and arrows, shows that they are men instead of belonging to the lower animals. Dr. Cook is going to write a full scientific account of these people.

PORTSMOUTH HERALD, AUGUST 17, 1899
NEW HAMPSHIRE GIANT NINE FEET TALL

Relics of a prehistoric age have been brought to light in Noble County. The find is in York Township where workmen excavating for a public highway found the skeleton of an inhabitant of early days.

The bones indicate that the person was fully nine feet tall. The bones are unusually large and the position of the skeleton when found indicated that the person had been buried in a sitting position.

The belief is advanced that the remains are those of a mound builder.

WASHINGTON BEE, NOVEMBER 4, 1899
THE VANISHED RACE
A BUILDING THAT HOUSED 6,000 CLIFF
DWELLERS

A Ruined Aboriginal City on a Cliff a Thousand Feet
High--Skulls of a People That Had Double Teeth All
Around—Some Remarkable Relics.

Laden with relics of the vanished race of the Cliff
Dwellers, the Rev. Dr. George L. Cole has returned
from a journey to the ruined cities of Southeastern
Colorado and New Mexico. Valuable results were
secured by excavations in an ancient communal
dwelling, as yet unnamed, which stands on the cliffs
of the Santa Fe River, fourteen miles from Espanola,
N. M. This is the largest pueblo yet discovered in the
United States, and Dr. Cole was practically the first to
visit it with scientific objects in view. He found stone
implements and pottery of extreme rarity, and the
bones of a race all of whose teeth were molars or
grinders. Among the bones excavated from a burial
mound on the mesa were a woman's femurs
measuring nineteen inches, a length which indicates
that this aboriginal giantess must have been at least
seven and a half feet tall. The cliff on which the
unexplored ruins stand rises a thousand feet above
the surrounding country. On one side of the isolated
rocky mass is the valley of the Santa Fe River, on the
other that of the Santa Clara. Up to 600 feet is a shelf

which furnished a nesting place for the Cliff Dwellers of nobody knows how many centuries ago. In the soft pumice stone they burrowed dens for their families. Eventually the original shelters in the cliffs grew to be a great warren. Room after room was hewn out until the rows were four or five deep. Under the shelter of the overhanging cliff, walls were built, extending the rows of rooms. The Cliff Dwellers were sheltered from rain or storm and their homes were inaccessible for their enemies.

Not satisfied with their rock caverns, the Cliff Dwellers climbed upward, and on the mesa, 400 feet above the shelf on which the caves opened, built a communal dwelling.

This mesa is about three-quarters of a mile wide and a mile and half long, which cliffs all about and the best opportunities for defense. On its edge was reared a watch tower of granite, whose height Dr. Cole believes to have been not less than sixty feet. The blocks were painfully carried up the 1,000-foot cliff, for the nearest granite deposits are at a considerable distance. For greater security a wall was built across the middle of the mesa.

On this rock platform, 1,000 feet up in the air, there stand to-day the ruins of two communal dwellings, one evidently much older than the other. The older dwelling is as yet untouched, and what little exploration of the more modern one Dr. Cole had time for amounts to a mere scratch on the surface.

There were not less than sixteen hundred rooms in the larger building in its prime, says Dr. Cole, and probably two thousand. The building measured 240x300 feet. It was blocks of stone measuring six by six by fifteen inches, quarried from the cliffs below, and carried up by the workmen. The rooms were roofed with timber, and the walls then carried higher. In the centre was a great court, a common kitchen for all, from which radiated immense numbers of rooms. The building spread with the growth of the community until it was three stories high and the rooms stretched away twelve deep from the central court, with smaller courts here and there. Dr. Cole estimates that the population averaged about three to a room, which would make between 4,800 and 6,000 people dwelling in the immense pueblo, besides those who lived in the cliff caves.

The rooms at the sides of the communal dwelling averaged about fourteen feet in size. On the upper stories they were mostly smaller, some being only seven by fourteen, others seven by twenty-one. Some rooms were found as large as fourteen by twenty-one feet.

With the trophies of his summer's explorations spread out about him, Dr. Cole has turned his parlor into an anthropological museum. One table is covered with water jugs and incense pipes, the sofa hidden under stone axes, mortars, pestles, weaving shuttles and pottery. Another table is decked with a row of grinning skulls and huge crossbones; beneath it comfortably repose all the parts of a skeleton, from the toe bones to the shoulder blades, waiting to be wired together, and strewn about are bows and arrows, baskets, jugs of twisted twigs, made watertight by pitch; modern Indian pottery, photographs by the score, and a stump of petrified wood. The skulls are a particularly valued possession.

"Look at those teeth," said Dr. Cole, tenderly fondling the skull of the giantess. "She has no incisors, no cutting teeth, in front, as have all the other races of which I have any knowledge. She has grinders all around, and so have the other skulls. That shows they were grain-eaters rather than meat-eaters. The foreheads are high and the shape of the skull shows intelligence, but notice how curiously they are flattened at the back.—Los Angeles Times.

WILLIAMSBURG, IOWA, JOURNAL TRIBUNE, APRIL 27, 1900
DOUBLE-TOOTHED GIANT

The discovery in Hardin County a short time ago by Joseph Booda and Elliot Charles Gaines of innumerable mound builders' relics, and the subsequent finding, by other parties, of the remains of a man of the prehistoric period, have greatly interested scientists in other parts of the country, the chief among these being Curator Charles Aldrich, of the state Horticultural Society.

Assuring himself of the truthfulness of the various newspaper reports, Mr. Aldrich has arranged to be in Eldora next month and begin a careful and systematic exploration of some of the mounds in the vicinity, the legal permission having been obtained.

In a large show window in Eldora for several days has been exhibited the skeleton of the man, which was found in a mound on the banks of the Iowa River, near Eagle City, six miles north. It has caused much interest and wonderment. Although well preserved, it is estimated that the skeleton is many centuries old. The skull is very large and thick, fully a quarter of an inch. A set of almost round double teeth are remarkably well preserved. They are yellow with age, are perfect in shape, and appear to have been double, both above and below. The femurs are very long showing a giant in stature.

Dr. N. C. Morse, a prominent physician who examined the skeleton, pronounced it that of a person who had evidently been trained for athletics, as the extremities were so well developed.

THE BOODA COLLECTION

Joseph Booda, who has taken much interest in mound exploration, has a rare collection of implements of the stone age, all found near Eldora. Among these are pottery axes, arrows, beadwork, pestles, mallets, and, although he has offers for the collection, will not part with it, unless he may be induced by Curator Aldrich to loan the collection to the state, to be placed in the historical building in Des Moines when completed.

1901-1910

NEW YORK TIMES, FEBRUARY 11, 1902
NEW MEXICO DISCOVERY: 12-FOOT GIANT
FOUND

Owing to the discovery of the remains of a race of giants in Guadalupe, New Mexico, antiquarians and archaeologists are preparing an expedition further to explore that region. This determination is based on the excitement that exists among the people of a scope of country near Mesa Rica, about 200 miles southeast of Las Vegas, where an old burial ground has been discovered that has yielded skeletons of enormous size. Luciana Quintana, on whose ranch the ancient burial plot is located, discovered two stones that bore curious inscriptions and beneath these were found in shallow excavations the bones of a frame that could not have been less than 12 feet in length. The men who opened the grave say the forearm was 4 feet long and that in a well-preserved jaw the lower teeth ranged from the size of a hickory nut to that of the largest walnut in size. The chest of the being is reported as having a circumference of seven feet. Quintana, who has uncovered many other burial places, expresses the opinion that perhaps thousands of skeletons of a race of giants long extinct, will be found. This supposition is based on the traditions handed down from the early Spanish invasion that have detailed knowledge of the existence of a race of giants that inhabited the plains of what now is Eastern New Mexico. Indian legends and carvings also in the same section indicate the existence of such a race.

THE ST. PAUL GLOBE, JANUARY 24, 1904
BONES OF A HUMAN SKELETON ELEVEN FEET
HIGH ARE DUG UP IN NEVADA

May Be Related to Cardiff Giant

WINNEMUCCA, Nev., Jan 23.—Workmen engaged in digging gravel here today uncovered at a depth of about twelve feet a lot of bones, part of a skeleton of a gigantic human being.

Dr. Samuels examined them and pronounced them to be the bones of a man who must have been nearly eleven feet in height.

The metacarpal bones measure four and a half inches in length and are large in proportion. A part of the ulna was found and in its complete form would have been between seventeen and eighteen inches in length.

The remainder of the skeleton is being searched for.

OHIO MORNING SUN NEWS HERALD, APRIL 14, 1904
ANOTHER OHIO GIANT NOW SEEMS SMALL AT ONLY EIGHT FEET

A giant skeleton of a man has been unearthed at the Woolverton farm, a short distance from Tippecanoe City, Ohio. It measures eight feet from the top of the head to the ankles, the feet being missing, says this newspaper reporter.

The skull is large enough to fit as a helmet over the average man's head. This skeleton was one of seven, buried in a circle, the feet of all being towards the center. Rude implements were near. The skeletons are thought to be those of mound builders.

BOSTON EVENING TRANSCRIPT, JUNE 12, 1906
OUR OWN ARCHAEOLOGY
A VALUABLE RELIC OF A FORMER AGE FOUND IN NEBRASKA, AND WHAT IT TELLS

Omaha World Herald – A find of the greatest archaeological interest was made some days ago a few feet back of the bungalow of Myron L. Learned, on the very top of the high bluff a half mile north of the village of Florence, by graders preparing for the foundations of an extension of the present building.

Under about two feet of vegetable mold and half a foot of loose deposit, of which the bluffs are formed, E. Wicke, the contractor doing the grading, plowed up what appears to be a stone spearhead. The implement, which is seven and one-quarter inches long from the extreme point of its base to its sharpened end and three inches wide at its widest point, is considered to be the most symmetrical and the best made ever found in the state.

Charles F. Crowley, professor of chemistry at Creighton Medical College, who is a practical geologist, also declares the implement to be made of flint but of a kind not native to this part of the United States.

One side of the stone is colored lustrous cobalt blue, while the reverse is white. Held to the light it is of a beautiful translucent rose orange. The chipping is evidently the work of a master in the art and the owner is greatly pleased at such a handsome and valuable addition to the stone implements which have been from time to time found about his summer cottage. The projectile point was found lying beside the teeth and larger bones of a bison, the inference being that its thrust had caused the death of the animal. An Omaha archaeologist who has examined the implement declares it to be an arrowhead, and he infers that it was probably used by one of the race of giants of which the legends of the Omaha tribe of Indians speak about. One of the tribal secret societies which has existed far back in the history of the nation tells of a people who preceded them in this section of the world, the males of which were ten or twelve feet high. Some ancient mounds opened in this vicinity have shown skeletons between eight and ten feet long, and he makes the deduction that if the projectile be an arrowhead its size indicates that the shaft into which it was originally fashioned was correspondingly large, and with so large an arrow, a bow with which it must be thrown would be too large for use by a man of ordinary stature. These deductions are conjectural, but the find must be regarded as a valuable one.

That human beings of enormous size inhabited this section of this country ages ago was proven last Sunday, when the massive skeleton of an Indian was unearthed near Pelican Lake. The interesting discovery was made by George Patton and L. H. Eaton, two Chicago tourists, who are spending the summer there.

For several days the men noticed a mound on their travels through the woods, and, at last led by curiosity, decided to excavate it. Procuring spades they fell to work and after digging down to a depth of about four feet were surprised to find the bones of a large human foot protruding through the earth.

Digging further, they gradually uncovered the perfect form of a giant. The skeleton was nearly 8 feet in height and the arms extended several inches below the hips. Buried with the bones were numerous stone weapons and trinkets. Among these were a curious stone hatchet, a copper knife, several strange copper rings, and a necklace made of the tusks of some prehistoric animal.

The skeleton is no doubt that of an Indian who was

one of a tribe of giants who roamed this part of the state over one thousand years ago.

NEW YORK TRIBUNE, FEBRUARY 3, 1909
SKELETON 15 FEET HIGH UNEARTHED IN
MEXICO

News was received here from Mexico that at Ixtapalapa, a town 10 mile southeast of Mexico City, there had been discovered what was believed to be the skeleton of a prehistoric giant of extraordinary size. A peon, while excavating for the foundation of a house on the estate of Augustin Juarez, found the skeleton of a human being that is estimated to have been about 15 feet high, and who must have lived ages ago, judging from the ossified state of the bones.

Romulo Luna, judge of the district, has taken possession of the skeleton which is complete with the exception of the skull.

Judge Luna says that as soon as the search for the skull is finished the skeleton will be forwarded to the national museum of Mexico that has an almost priceless collection of Aztec antiquities.

PORTLAND, OREGON SUNDAY OREGONIAN, MARCH 13, 1910
PREHISTORIC MAN'S BONES ARE FOUND

Skeleton 10 Feet Long Discovered in Southern Idaho Cave

PART OF A GUN ALSO TAKEN

Members of Hunting Party Making Strange Find.

Cannot Identify Rusty Barrel Among Known Firearms—To Move Bones

BOISE, Idaho, March 12.—(Special)—Unmoved, unseen and untouched for hundreds of years and hidden in the recesses of a deep cave 25 miles north of Shoshone, Lincoln County in Southern Idaho, is the skeletons of a giant, ten feet tall evidently of prehistoric origin. It was recently discovered by a hunting party from this city.

As corroborated proof the members are now exhibiting the rusty and worn flint lock barrel of what appears to be an ancient gun weighing between 25 and 30 pounds, resembling a flit-lock rifle. This they say was picked up beside the skeleton.

These bones will be taken out of the cave at the earliest possible date and carefully packed and forwarded to the Smithsonian Institution. It is believed by those who have seen the skeleton there will be an invasion of the caves in that section of Idaho by students seeking knowledge of the earlier inhabitants of America.

Skull of Great Size.

The skull of this giant is twice as large as that of the average man today. The large limb bones indicate that he must have been a man of great physical power. The skeleton is well preserved and was found upon the surface of the ground far back in the chambers of the cave, stretched out at full length. Close by was the barrel of the rusty rifle, which is of peculiar make unknown to those familiar with firearms.

No reasonable theory can be advanced by the discovery as to how the skeleton happened to be in the cave. Those who have looked into the facts believe the skeleton represents one of a lost race unknown to men of this day, which occupied the American continent long before the redskins came. Geologists say the Western country was the scene of a great volcanic disturbance at one time and great streams of lava overflowed the now fertile plains of this state, forming caves and great natural basins. It is possible that this one representative of a lost race was caught by the flows and sealed up in the cave in which he was found.

Extinct Volcanoes Abound.

There are numerous extinct volcanoes in this section of the state and particularly where the gigantic skeleton was found. The older Indians say their fathers told them about the mountains which were afire and of the continual underground rumblings. Among the "lavas," as these regions are called, are tobe found many fissures that seem to be connected with large caves, formed when the lava was cooling, and at times the suction is so great at the mouth of these fissures that large papers thrown into them are immediately sucked downwards, while at other times the current of air is outward and can be heard for

miles on a frosty morning. Few people care to enter the caves but those which have large openings on the surface are considered perfectly safe.

1911-1920

BELVIDERE DAILY REPUBLICAN, APRIL 12, 1911
FIND INDIAN RELICS NEAR LAKE DELAVAN
Fourteen Are Unearthed Beneath Knoll Where
Chicagoans Camp.

Lake Delavan, Wisconsin – Out of a knoll that for years has formed the playground of thousands of Chicago people during the summer months, Phillips Bros., owners of Lake Lawn farm, have just dug fourteen human skeletons, and the probability is that still other finds will be unearthed.

For years it has been suspected that the big mound on which several Chicago church choirs have been accustomed to camp, one after another, in different years, contained rich Indian relics, but no one seemed to make a move toward exploration.

As the result of an argument as to what was hidden in the mound, the owners of the place dug down eight feet and raked out skeletons which are probably the largest specimens of the red race found in southern Wisconsin. Two of the skeletons were found in a sitting posture. All were buried in a stone-floored and walled pit, over which a solid clay slab had been placed.

The skeletons have been preserved intact and will go to the state museum at Madison.

Walworth county has a very large number of the mounds, some of them having been explored, with the result that only a few relics, most of them crude weapons, were found.

OAKLAND TRIBUNE, JULY 25, 1911
BONES OF SEVEN FOOT CALIFORNIAN GIANT
FOUND IN SOUTH

Ethnologists will be interested in a discovery made by Assistant Curator William Altmann of Golden Gate Park Memorial Museum—namely, the fact hitherto denied that the Digger Indians of California were acquainted with at least the rudiments of pottery making. "Until now, no pottery of Digger Indian manufacture has ever been found," says Altmann, and therefore he highly values the find he made in an Indian Burial Mound at Concord, in Contra Costa County.

From an excavation made by workmen in the employ of the Port Costa Water Company has been found a large number of Indian relics of great age, including the specimens of crude pottery already mentioned and the skeleton of an Indian giant more than seven feet tall. The skeleton is in the possession of Dr. Neff of Concord, who is mounting it for exhibition. The pottery specimens consist of charm stones of baked clay of spindle shape and pierced so that they may be suspended from the neck by cords.

In addition, there are a large number of knives and arrowheads of obsidian or volcanic glass, which is extremely rare in this part of the state, and leads to the belief they were brought down by the Shasta or

Modoc Indians and traded for other things with the Diggers of Contra Costa.

A striking peculiarity about these arrowheads is their shape and pattern. They are notched in a very painstaking way with jagged division and resemble very much some of the weapons Filipino warriors use. A stone mortar and several phallic pestles carved with considerable skill and precision, stone sinkers for fishing, and artistic pipes made of soapstone, together with a quantity of wampum, are among the souvenirs secured by Assistant Curator Altmann, the donor being Joseph Hittman of Concord.

The mound from which these relics were taken is close to the railroad depot at Concord. The work of excavation is still going on and more interesting finds are looked for.

ARIZONA JOURNAL-MINER, OCTOBER 13, 1911
RANCHER REFUSES TO SELL SKELETON OF
GIANT

Peter Marx of Walnut Creek, discoverer of a prehistoric human giant on his farm several weeks ago, while in the city yesterday, stated that the curiosity is attracting such deep interest in scientific circles that he is almost delayed with his letters and during the past two weeks he has been visited by Mr. and Mrs. Shoup, the former an attaché of the Smithsonian Institution at Washington, who made the long journey for the express purpose of viewing the frame of the giant of other days. Mr. Shoup was provided with photographic instruments and took several pictures.

Mr. Shoup, of the Smithsonian, also desired to take it (the giant skeleton) back to Washington, but this request was held up by Mr. Marx stating that as the subject was found in the territory it should be kept there.

Mr. Shoup was very much interested in those portions of the human frame that were unusually large, particularly the skull, which indicated that the giant was of such abnormal size as to be beyond comprehension as that of a human being. Mr. Marx has uncovered another burying ground near the point where the skeleton was found.

IRRIGATION DITCHES ARE A SIGN OF ANCIENT HIGH INTELLIGENCE

An old irrigating ditch has also been partly recovered, and it is Mr. Shoup's (of the Smithsonian) belief that the place was intelligently cultivated in some past age by an industrious people. Mr. Marx has uncovered many implements, some of which are unique in construction and for what purposes they were utilized is problematical.

ALTON EVENING TELEGRAPH, MAY 4, 1912
BONES OF OLD RACE FOUND.

Skeletons Discovered in Wisconsin Are Larger Than Present Men.

Madison, Wis., May 3. – Examination of a score of skeletons discovered in mounds at Lake Delavan and Lake Lawn Farm was declared today to indicate that a hitherto unknown race of men inhabited Southern Wisconsin ages ago. Information of the characteristics of the skeletons was brought to Madison today by Attorney Maurice Morrissey, of Delavan, and Charles E. Brown, curator of the State Historical Museum, will make a further investigation.

The heads are very much larger than those of any people which inhabit America today. From directly over the eye sockets, however, the head slopes straight back and the nasal bones protrude far above the cheek bones. The jaw bones are long and pointed, resembling those of an ape.

Skeletons supposed to be those of women had smaller heads, which were similar in facial characteristics.

The skeletons are embedded in charcoal from 4 to 10 feet deep and covered over with layers of baked clay, designed, it is believed, to shed water from the sepulcher.

Note: Various versions of this story ran in newspapers across the country.

MILWAUKEE SENTINEL, JUNE 8, 1912
PRIMITIVE MAN A GIANT
From the Seattle Post-Intelligence.

Eleven skeletons of primitive men, with foreheads sloping directly back from the eyes, and with two rows of teeth in the front of the upper jaw, have been uncovered in Craigshill, at Ellensburg, this state. They were found about twenty feet below the surface, twenty feet back from the face of the slope, in a cement rock formation over which was a layer of shale. The rock was perfectly dry.
The jaw bones, which easily break, are so large that they will go around the face of the man of today. The other bones are also much larger than those of the ordinary man. The femur is twenty inches long, indicating, scientists say, a man eighty inches tall.
J. P. Munson, professor of biology in the state normal school, who lectured before the International

biological college in Austria last summer, visited the spot and pronounced them the bones of a primitive man. The teeth in front are worn almost down to the jaw bones, due, Dr. Munson says, to eating uncooked foods and crushing hard substances with the teeth. The sloping skull, he says, shows an extremely low order of intelligence, far earlier than that of the Indians known to the whites.

(Note: This version of the article was widely reprinted over the following months)

OAKLAND TRIBUNE, JUNE 10, 1912
BEST-PRESERVED SKELETON OF EXTINCT TRIBE
HAULED FROM CHANNEL

Up to about three hundred years ago, a giant race inhabited the coastal regions of California. Remains of these people have been discovered in the islands of the Santa Barbara Channel. To William Altmann, assistant curator of the Golden Gate Park Memorial Museum, belongs the honor of discovering one of the tallest and best preserved skeletons of this extinct tribe. Altmann utilized his vacation a week ago in excavating an old Indian burial mound in the nursery of Thomas S. Duane, two miles from Concord, in Contra Costa County.

The giant skeleton found was ten feet from the

surface and around it were a large number of mortars and pestles, charm stones, and obsidian arrow heads. The giant skeleton has been laid and reconstructed in the Curator's office and placed on private exhibition yesterday. The bones are in a good state of preservation, being hard and firm, although brown with age. Two or three of the vertebrae are missing and the skull is broken into three parts.

The skeleton is seven feet four inches. The skull is in great contrast to that of the Indian today. The under-jaw is square and massive, being remarkably thick and strong.

PHALLIC CARVINGS

The artifacts are ornamented with phallic carvings, whereas the marks made by the former and present-day Diggers are not carved or ornamented in any way. The charm stones are of baked clay, a beginning of the more advanced works of pottery, which are not found with Digger remains. This interesting find was made on the Salvadore Pacheen Ranch, part of which is occupied by Duane's nursery. It is Altmann's intention to make a further exploration of the mound at an early [date] for other relics of this by-gone era.

A SUPERIOR RACE OF GIANTS ADMITTED IN CALIFORNIA

The find is of the greatest importance to anthropologists the world over, confirming as it does, the theory originally advanced when the giants were unearthed in the Santa Barbara Islands, that a superior race of Indians, both physically and mentally, preceded the Digger and other native races of the present day. This is evidenced also in the burial posture and the charm stones found near the body.

LOGANSPORT PHAROS TRIBUNE, JUNE 19, 1912
DOUBLE DENTITIONS

Charles Milton found a skeleton that is thought to be that of an Indian while digging sand near Lake Cleott yesterday. The bones are well preserved and very large. The jaw bone is almost twice as large as that of the ordinary person.

One peculiarity about the jaw is the fact that the teeth are double both front and back. The sandpit where the bones were found is supposed to be an old Indian mound. Several arrow heads were excavated and other like utensils were found. Among these was a peculiarly shaped flint supposed to have been a fish scaler. About two or three bushels of charcoal was found along the side of the skeleton.

MORNING REVIEW, SEPTEMBER 4, 1912
BONES OF ANCIENT GIANT
Amazing Discovery in Oregon is of Great Interest to Anthropologists

The discovery of the bones of a human giant at Ellensburg is one of the most interesting anthropological finds made in the northwest, according to L. L. Sharp, chief of the general land office. "I just returned from Ellensburg," said he, "where I had opportunity to view the bones unearthed. The skull, jawbone, thigh and other parts of the largest skeleton indicated a man to my mind of at least eight feet high. A man of his stature and massive frame would weigh fully 300 pounds at least. The head is one of the most remarkable I ever have studied among prehistoric skulls. It is massive, with enormous brain space. While the forehead slopes down somewhat, not averaging the abrupt eminence of our present race, the width between the ears and the deep, well-rounded space at the back of the head are convincing testimony of high intelligence for a primitive man. The cheekbones are not high, like those of the Indian, nor has the head any resemblance to the Indian skull. I am convinced that this skull is of a prehistoric man who was one of a remarkable race of people who inhabited this part of American some time prior to the Indian control.

"The bones were uncovered fully 20 feet beneath the

surface. There is the usual gravel formation on top, then the conglomerate, a stratum of shale, and in a bed of concrete gravel beneath the shale were the bones of the giant and of a smaller person. The shale would indicate tremendous age, perhaps more than 1,000,000 years, for the deposit in which the skeleton was found. But this I deem impossible, and presume that the bones were put beneath the shale by means of a tunnel perhaps, or some other system of interment. I cannot think it possible that a human being of the advanced stage indicated by this great skull could have existed at the period when the shale was formed."—Portland (Ore.) Telegram.

LA CROSSE TRIBUNE, NOVEMBER 4, 1912
FIFTY SKELETONS UNEARTHED--REMAINS OF
GIANT ABORIGINES DISCOVERED

More than fifty skeletons of the ancient mound builders were unearthed Saturday from five mounds in the town of Stoddard, by a party of Normal students and professors, who made a special trip to investigate them. Valuable relics were also recovered that will be on exhibition at the Normal museum.
The country around La Crosse has long been known as the center of Indian activities in centuries long past and as evidences of this fact there are many Indian mounds in this vicinity.

About thirty years ago agents of the Smithsonian Institution in Washington D.C., investigated several mounds in what is now the town of Stoddard. They unearthed much valuable material in the line of skeletons, arrow heads, and spear heads from the first few of a chain of a dozen mounds and at the present time there is in Washington a Stoddard Collection of Indian relics.

Since that time Smithsonian officials have often considered opening more of the mounds but nothing has been done. Spurred on by the generous offer of A. White, who owns the ground on which are located five large mounds, to donate the contents to the Normal School Museum (apparently no help from Smithsonian officials), the Normal authorities recently took the matter up, and several local citizens generously provided a fund for the expenses of an expedition to unearth the contents.

A SIX-FOOT, SIX-INCH SKELETON UNEARTHED
Professors A. H. Sanford and W. H. Thompson of the University of Wisconsin Department of History, and L. P. Deneyer of the Geology Department, together with a company of thirteen students left on Saturday morning with shovels to examine the ancient graves. Professor Austin and some of his students surveyed and made a contour map of the field determining the dimensions of the mounds and the lay of the surrounding country. The expedition was of a

scientific character, and the results of the investigations will appear in printed form.

A large mound in the center, probably the grave of an Indian chief, was adjoined by two smaller ones on each side. The latter were investigated first and the efforts of the diggers were rewarded at once by the unearthing of a skeleton about five feet down, which measured six and a half feet in length.
The skull was very large being eight inches in diameter from ear to ear. The teeth were well preserved, but the other bones quickly fell to pieces. The first mound yielded eleven skeletons. The second contained only charcoal and burned bones indicating cremation.

EFFORTS YIELD MANY SKELETONS AND ARTIFACTS
The middle mound, which was the largest, required much effort to excavate. More than twenty skeletons were found besides the bowl of a clay peace pipe, a copper arrow head, copper skinning knife, a sandstone spearhead, and several flint arrow heads. The fourth eminence yielded over twenty five skeletons, pieces of clay pottery, and a bear's tooth.
The last mound, after digging about six feet down, brought up a large spear point of quartz with a red coloring design on each side. Adjoining the White farm is property owned by Homer Hart of La Crosse on which are located several more mounds.

MONROE COUNTY MAIL, JUNE 18, 1914
SCIENTISTS FIND GIANT SKELETON: IN LIFE
THEY AVERAGED TWELVE FEET HIGH

Skeletons of a race of giants who averaged twelve feet in height were found by workmen engaged on a drainage project in Crowville, near here.

There are several score at least of the skeletons, and they lie in various positions. It is believed they were killed in a prehistoric fight and that the bodies lay where they fell until covered with alluvial deposits due to the flooding of the Mississippi River. No weapons of any sort were found at the site, and it is believed the Titans must have struggled with wooden clubs. The skulls are in a perfect state of preservation, and some of the jawbones are large enough to surround a baby's body.

EL PASO HERALD, APRIL 19, 1915
ARIZONA GIANTS

"The skeleton of a giant fully eight feet tall has been found near Silver City," said H. E. Davis. The thigh bone of this ancient inhabitant of the southwest measures two inches more than the ordinary man and must have been a giant of great strength. The jaw bone is large enough to fit over the jaw of an ordinary man. A peculiarity of the forehead is that it recedes from the eyes like that of an ape. The similarity is still further found in the sharp bones under the eyes. The skeleton was found encased in baked mud, indicating that encasing the corpse in mud and baking it was the mode of embalming. Near the skeleton was found a stone weighing 12 pounds, which, judging from its shape, must have been a club. The wooden handle has rotted away but there are marks on the stone that indicate that it had been bound to a wooden handle with tongs. It is rather peculiar that less than 30 miles from where this skeleton was found and located on the Gile river are the former houses of a tribe of small cliff dwellers. The existence of these two races so near together forms an interesting topic. "These 'gorillalike' or 'monkey-like' skulls have been reported in many states several times by Smithsonian personnel. Professor Thomas Wilson, the curator of Prehistoric Anthropology for the Smithsonian, said the following about the find of an eight-foot-one-inch giant skeleton in Miamisburg, Ohio, in 1897. "The authenticity of the skull is beyond doubt. Its antiquity is unquestionably great. To my own personal knowledge several such crania were discovered in the Hopewell group of mounds in Ohio, exhibiting monkey-like traits."

LOS ANGELES TIMES, SEPTEMBER 3, 1916
FIND BONES OF GIANT IN A CALIFORNIA CAVE

The discovery of a skull, jawbones and femur of giant proportions by D. L. Gilliland and F. M. Puntenney of Moonpark, in a cavern in one of the canyons of the great Pisgah Grando Rancho just over the Ventura county line, lends color to the belief, long held by residents of that scenic section, that the burying place of a prehistoric race of giants has been found. The find was made under peculiar circumstances, Messrs Gilliland and Puntenney who are officers of the law at Moonpark, were searching for two Mexicans, said to have been connected with robberies at Moonpark and Santa Susana. After scouring the various canyons they came upon a wide cavern deep in the brush and hidden from view by a rugged rampart of rocks.

Seeing that there was an opening in which the fugitives might take shelter, Mr. Puntenney pulled aside the underbrush and peered into the depths. Within he saw the grinning skull of huge size and the great femur, that must have formed the thigh bone of a mighty giant. In this vast and silent region are to be seen ancient ruins that still stand in mute testimony of the fact that at some remote period in the history of our sunny Southland a race of giants lived and moved and had their being. And that in these small but fertile valleys, this long forgotten race built their crude homes and practiced the arts of life according to their original lights.The skull, jawbones and femur of the giant's skeleton found by Messrs Gilliland and Puntenney, were brought to Moonpark in an office in that town, where examined by Dr. Philo Hull, who has pronounced them unquestionably those of a human being. The bones are being preserved and are on exhibition, they are attracting a great deal of attention.

CHARLESTON DAILY MAIL, SEPTEMBER 20, 1916
REPORT OF SIXTY-EIGHT SKELETONS
AVERAGING SEVEN-FEET TALL

On July 13, Professor Skinner of the American Indian Museum, excavating the mound at Tioga Point, near Sayre, Pennsylvania, uncovered the bones of 68 men, which he estimates had been buried at least seven or eight hundred years. The average height indicated by the skeletons was seven feet, but many were taller. Evidence of the gigantic size of these men was seen in huge axes found beside the bones.

Some large mounds have been found in this territory. In some places a number of pieces of pottery have been unearthed. It will be remembered that when the dam at International Falls was under construction several hundred pieces of tempered copper were unearthed from a depth of 15 feet. The articles consisted of fish hooks, knives, spears, and arrows. The art of tempering copper, which was known by these early mound builders, is now a lost art. An unusually large skeleton was also unearthed and thought to have been a woman. Physicians who have examined the skeleton declare that it represented a type of early prehistoric persons who were seven feet tall or more and who possessed an especially large lower jaw. They drew this conclusion because the skeleton found was that of a person of very large stature. The jaw bone was wide and its construction is said to be a special gift of nature to the early man in order that he could masticate the coarser foods which then made up his subsistence. The skull is very large. The well rounded forehead gives evidence of considerable development of intelligence of the Rainy Lake territory. [...] The skeleton will be sent to the Minnesota Historical Society.

PHILADELPHIA INQUIRER, NOVEMBER 22, 1920
THE CARNEGIE MUSEUM CLAIMS POSSESSION OF AN EIGHT- TO NINE-FOOT GIANT

Dr. W. J. Holland curator of the Carnegie Museum, Pittsburgh and his assistant Dr. Peterson, a few days ago opened up a mound of the ancient race that inhabited this state and secured the skeleton, who, while in the flesh, was from 8–9 feet in height.

The mound was originally about 100 feet long and more than 12 feet high somewhat worn down by time. It is on the J. B. Secrest farm in South Huntington Township. This farm has been in the Secrest name for more than a century. The most interesting feature in the recent excavations were the mummified torso of a human body, which the experts figured was laid to rest at least 400 years ago.

"Portions of the bones dug up and the bones in the leg," Prof. Peterson declares, "are those of a person between eight and nine feet in height." The scientist figures that this skeleton was the framework of a person of the prehistoric race that inhabited this area before the American Indian. The torso and the portions of the big skeleton were shipped to the Carnegie Museum. Dr. Holland and Peterson supervised the explorations of the mound with the greatest of care. The curators believe the man whose skeleton they secured belonged to the mound builder class.

THE VANCOUVER SUN, AUGUST 18, 1922
PRIMITIVE MAN, TEN FEET TALL, IS UNEARTHED

MEXICO CITY, Aug. 17 – The department of agriculture received yesterday from an agent on Tiburon Island, Gulf of California, the skeleton of a primitive man, more than ten feet tall. It was found a few days ago. Other bones of similar size have been encountered.

THE NEW YORK TIMES, AUGUST 19, 1922
STONE AGE CONNECTICUT
Prehistoric Inhabitants of Nutmeg State Were Flat-Heads of Great Strength and Huge Teeth

BRIDGEPORT, Conn., Aug 19.--Two complete skeletons, believed to have belonged to inhabitants of the earth in the Stone Age, are said to have been unearthed by a band of archaeologists, headed by Prof. Warren King Moorehead, near the Housatonic River, at Laurel Beach.

The professor and his assistants have been digging in this section for some time and claim discovery of a number of indications that the section was once inhabited by a forgotten race.

Both skeletons appear to be well preserved. The

bones are rough, denoting great strength, the skulls are flat and both possess a perfect set of teeth of unusual size.

Prof. Moorehead said it was his belief the bodies were buried in salt water several thousand years ago, which accounts for their preservation. He also expressed the hope that he and his assistants would soon locate a burial ground of a tribe of an ancient race.

SKELETON OF A GIANT FOUND.—A day or two since, some workmen engaged in subsoiling the grounds of Sheriff WICKHAM, at his vineyard in East Wheeling, came across a human skeleton. Although much decayed, there was little difficulty in identifying it, by placing the bones, which could not have belonged to others than a human body, in their original position. The impression made by the skeleton in the earth, and the skeleton itself, were measured by the Sheriff and a brother in the craft *locale*, both of whom were prepared to swear that it was *ten feet nine inches in length*. Its jaws and teeth were almost as large as those of a horse. The bones are to be seen at the Sheriff's office.—*Wheeling Times.*

Reported Discovery of a Huge Skeleton.

From the Sank Rapids (Minn.) Sentinel, Dec. 18.

Day before yesterday, while the quarrymen employed by the Sank Rapids Water Power Company were engaged in quarrying rock for the dam which is being erected across the Mississippi, at this place, found imbedded in the solid granite rock the remains of a human being of gigantic stature. About seven feet below the surface of the ground, and about three feet and a half beneath the upper stratum of rock, the remains were found imbedded in the sand, which had evidently been placed in the quadrangular grave which had been dug out of the solid rock to receive the last remains of this antideluvian giant. The grave was twelve feet in length, four feet wide, and about three feet in depth, and is to-day at least two feet below the present level of the river. The remains are completely petrified, and are of gigantic dimensions. The head is massive, measures thirty-one and one-half inches in circumference, but low in the *asfrontis*, and very flat on top. The Femur measures twenty-six and a quarter inches, and the Fibula twenty-five and a half, while the body is equally long in proportion. From the crown of the head to the sole of the foot, the length is ten feet nine and a half inches. The measure around the chest is thirty-nine and a half inches. The giant must have weighed at least 900 pounds when covered with a reasonable amount of flesh. The petrified remains, and there is nothing left but the naked bones, now weigh 304¼ pounds. The thumb and fingers of the left hand, and the left foot from the ankle to the toes are gone; but all the other parts are perfect. Over the sepulchre of the unknown dead was placed a large flat limestone rock that remained perfectly separated from the surrounding granite rock.

The New York Times
Published: December 25, 1868

More Big Indians Found in Virginia.

Not to be behind Canada, Virginia puts in a claim of the possession of a cave full of dead Indians, the Petersburg *Index* giving the tale as quoted below, on the authority of gentlemen whom it asserts to be of the highest character and credit. who have seen with their own eyes, and touched and tested with their own hands, the wonderful objects of which they make report as follows:

"The workmen engaged in opening a way for the projected railroad between Weldon and Garysburg struck Monday, about one mile from the former place, in a bank beside the river, a catacomb of skeletons, supposed to be those of Indians, of a remote age and a lost and forgotten race. The bodies exhumed were of strange and remarkable formation. The skulls were nearly an inch in thickness; the teeth were filed sharp, as are those of cannibals, the enamel perfectly preserved; the bones were of wonderful length and strength—the *femur* being as long as the leg of an ordinary man, the stature of the body being, probably, as great as eight or nine feet. Near their heads were sharp stone arrows, stone mortars, in which their corn was brayed, and the bowls of pipes, apparently of soft friable soap-stone. The teeth of the skeletons are said to be as large as those of horses. One of them has been brought to the city, and presented to an officer of the Petersburg Railroad. The bodies were found closely packed together, laid tier on tier as it seemed. There was no discernable ingress into or egress out of the mound."

The New York Times

Published: September 8, 1871

TWO VERY TALL SKELETONS.
From the Harrisburg (Penn) Telegraph.

The following was copied verbatim from a note made in his pocket almanac by the late Judge Atlee: "On the 24th of May, 1798, being at Hanover (York County, Penn.,) in company with Chief-Justice McKean, Judge Bryan, Mr. Burd, and others, on our way to Franklin, and, taking a view of the town, in company with Mr. McAlister, and several other respectable inhabitants, we went to Mr. Neese's tan-yard, where we were shown a place near the currying-house from whence (in digging to sink a tan-vat) some years ago were taken two skeletons of human bodies. They lay close beside each other, and measured about 11 feet 3 inches in length; the bones were entire, but on being taken up and exposed to the air they presently crumbled and fell to pieces. Mr. McAlister and some others mentioned that they and many others had seen them, and Mr. McAlister, who is a tall man, about 6 feet 4 inches high, mentioned that the principal bone of the leg of one of them, being placed by the side of his leg, reached from his ankle a considerable way up his thigh, pointing a small distance below the hip bone."

THE BONES OF A GIANT FOUND.

ST. PAUL, Minn., May 24.—A skull of heroic size and singular formation has been discovered among the relics of the mound-builders in the Red River Valley. The mound was 60 feet in diameter and 12 feet high. Near the centre were found the bones of about a dozen men and women, mixed with the bones of various animals. The skull in question was the only perfect one, and near it were found some abnormally large body bones. The man who bore it was evidently a giant. A thorough investigation of the mound and its contents will be made by the Historical Society.

The New York Times

Published: May 25, 1882

A GIANT'S REMAINS IN A MOUND.

From the Charleston (West Va.) Call.

Prof. Norris, the ethnologist, who has been examining the mounds in this section of West Virginia for several months, the other day opened the big mound on Col. B. H. Smith's farm, six or eight miles below here. This is the largest mound in the valley and proved a rich store-house. The mound is 50 feet high, and they dug down to the bottom. It was evidently the burial place of a noted chief, who had been interred with unusual honors. At the bottom they found the bones of a human being, measuring 7 feet in length and 19 inches across the shoulders. He was lying flat, and at either side, lying at an angle of about 45 degrees, with their feet pointed toward their chief, were other men, on one side two and on the other three. At the head of the chief lay another man, with his hands extended before him, and bearing two bracelets of copper. On each side of the chief's wrists were six copper bracelets, while a looking-glass of mica lay at his shoulder and a gorget of copper rested on his breast. Four copper bracelets were under his head, with an arrow in the centre. A house 12 feet in diameter and 10 feet high, with a ridge pole 1 foot in diameter, had been erected over them, and the whole covered by the dirt that formed the mound. Each of the men buried there had been inclosed in a bark coffin.

The New York Times
Published: November 20, 1883
Copyright © The New York Times

MUST HAVE BEEN GOLIATH.

Hon. J. H. Hainly, a well-known and reliable citizen of Barnard, Mo., writes to the St. Joseph *Gazette* the particulars of the discovery of a giant skeleton four miles southwest of that place. A farmer named John W. Hannon found the bones protruding from the bank of a ravine that has been cut by the action of the rains during the past years. Mr. Hannon worked several days in unearthing the skeleton, which proved to be that of a human being, whose height was twelve feet. The head through the temple was twelve inches; from the lower part of the skull at the back was fifteen inches, and the circumference forty inches. The ribs were nearly four feet long and one and three-quarter inches wide. The thigh bones were thirty inches long and large in proportion. When the earth was removed the ribs stood up high enough to enable a man to crawl in and explore the interior of the skeleton, turn around and come out with ease. The first joint of the great toe, above the nail, was three inches long, and the entire foot eighteen inches in length. The skeleton lay on its face, twenty feet below the surface of the ground, and the toes were imbedded in the earth, indicating that the body either fell or was placed there when the ground was soft. The left arm was passed around backward, the hand resting on the spinal column, while the right arm was stretched out to the front and right. Some of the bones crumbled on exposure to the air, but many good specimens were preserved and are now on exhibition at Barnard. Medical men are much interested. The skeleton is generally pronounced a valuable relic of the prehistoric race.

SKELETONS SEVEN FEET LONG.

CENTREBURG, Ohio, May 4.—Licking County has been for years a favorite field for students of Indian history, there being here two old forts and scores of mounds. Last week a small mound near Homer was opened by some schoolboys, who found a skeleton. To-day further search was made, and several feet below the surface of the earth in a large vault, with stone floor and bark covering, were found four huge skeletons, three being each over seven feet in length and the other eight. The skeletons lay with their feet to the east on a bed of charcoal in which were numerous partially burned bones. About the neck of the largest skeleton were a lot of stone beads, evidently a necklace in life. The grave contained about 30 stone vessels and implements, the most striking being a curiously wrought pipe, the bowl having a series of carved figures upon it representing a contest between animals and birds. It is said to be the only engraved stone pipe ever found. A stone kettle holding about a gallon, in which was a residue of saline matter, bears evidence of much skill. Their bows, a number of arrows, stone hatchets, and a stone knife are among the implements. The knife is of peculiar shape, with a curved blade and wooden handle. Students of Indian archæology claim it is the most valuable find ever made in that line.

The New York Times
Published: May 5, 1885

A RACE OF INDIAN GIANTS.

MAY'S LANDING. N. J., Feb. 8.—For over a week past crowds have been flocking to the site of the unearthed Indian graveyard near Edgewater-avenue in Pleasantville. The first lot of skeletons unearthed was about one thousand yards from the city Post Office and embraced eight bodies, closely laid together in a deep chamber, snugly packed in with tortoise, oyster, and clam shells. One of this number had bead and shell decorations, which, together with its extreme height, points to the fact that it must have been the powerful old chief Kineawaugha, whose descendants still own farms along the shore.

Prof. C. H. Farrel of Baltimore, Charles K. Simpson of New-York. John H. Cooley, Jr., of New-Haven, Conn., and several gentlemen from the University of Pennsylvania immediately went to the scene. Messrs. Risley and Farr, the owners of the land, gave to the Archæological Association of the University of Pennsylvania the right to search for relics on their land. These researches have been watched by thousands of people with great interest. Besides weapons of war savage ornamental war decorations and numerous valuable shells. stones, &c., over fifty skeletons have been exhumed.

Dr. Charles R. Abbott, curator of the association, is continuing the search, and the skeletons are to be shipped to the university at once. They run in size from a small child to several of seven feet in height, and one, supposed to be an old medicine man, Wauneck, must have been at least eight feet in height. About fifty students were upon the ground this morning and continued their search until stopped by rain.

The citizens gaze in silent wonder on these relics of a race that at one time ruled the land. For seven miles along the shore can be seen large mounds of clam and oyster shells left here by Indians who used to congregate by hundreds to open oysters for Winter food, and it is near these shell mounds that the great number of skeletons have been taken up. In some instances weapons of war made of stone and flint have been found lying close beside some exceedingly large skeletons. The relics will be put on exhibition at the museum of the university in Philadelphia.

The New York Times
Published: February 9, 1890

Further investigation of the Sweeny mounds, near Carthage, Ill., resulted in the unearthing of hundreds of ▓▓▓▓ ▓▓▓▓▓ of ▓▓▓▓ proportions.

Dodge City times., September 11, 1891

Two ▓▓▓▓ ▓▓▓▓▓ ▓▓▓▓▓▓▓ Found.

BEAVER FALLS, Aug. 22.—[*Special.*]—Workmen, while digging a ditch from the new shovel works to the river at Alliquippa to-day, unearthed the remains of two skeletons. They are of gigantic size, and are supposed to be the remains of two Indians. They have been in the ground for many years, as the larger bones and skull only remain.

Pittsburg dispatch., August 23, 1892

A Race of Giants in Old Gaul.

From the London Globe.

In the year 1890 some human bones of enormous size, double the ordinary in fact, were found in the tumulus of Castelnau, (Hérault,) and have since been carefully examined by Prof. Kiener, who, while admitting that the bones are those of a very tall race, nevertheless finds them abnormal in dimensions and apparently of morbid growth. They undoubtedly reopen the question of the "giants" of antiquity, but do not furnish sufficient evidence to decide it.

The New York Times
Published: October 3, 1892
Copyright © The New York Times

UNEARTH SKELETON OF GIANT

Bones of Supposed Mound Builder Those of Man Eight or Nine Feet High.

Dr. W. J. Holland, curator of the Carnegie museum, Pittsburgh, and his assistant, Dr. Peterson, a few days ago opened up a mound of the ancient race that inhabited this section and secured the skeleton of a man who when in the flesh was between eight and nine feet in height, says a Greensburg (Pa.) dispatch to the Philadelphia Inquirer.

This mound, which was originally about 100 feet long and more than 12 feet high, has been somewhat worn down by time. It is on the J. R. Secrist farm in South Huntingdon township. This farm has been in the Secrist name for more than a century.

The most interesting feature in the recent excavation was the mummified torso of the human body, which the experts figured was laid to rest at least 400 years ago. Portions of the bones dug up and the bones in the legs, Prof. Peterson declares, are those of a person between eight and nine feet in height. The scientist figures that this skeleton was the framework of a person of the prehistoric race that inhabited this section before the American Indians.

The torso and the portions of the big skeleton were shipped to the Carnegie museum. Drs. Holland and Peterson supervised the explorations on the Secrist mound with the greatest of care. The curators believe the man whose skeleton they secured belonged to the mound builder class.

The sun., December 08, 1893,

GIANTS OF OTHER DAYS.

Recent Discoveries Near Serpent Mound, Ohio.

From The Indianapolis Journal.

Farmer Warren Cowen of Hillsborough, Ohio, while fox hunting recently discovered several ancient graves. They were situated upon a high point of land in Highland County, Ohio, about a mile from the famous Serpent Mound, where Prof. Putnam of Harvard made interesting discoveries. As soon as the weather permitted, Cowen excavated several of these graves. The graves were made of large limestone slabs, two and a half to three feet in length and a foot wide. These were set on edge about a foot apart. Similar slabs covered the graves. A single one somewhat larger was at the head and another at the foot. The top of the grave was two feet below the present surface.

Upon opening one of the graves a skeleton upward of six feet in length was brought to light. There were a number of stone hatchets, beads, and ornaments of peculiar workmanship near the right arm. Several large flint spear and arrow heads among the ribs gave evidence that the warrior had died in battle.

In another grave was the skeleton of a man equally large. The right leg had been broken during life, and the bones had grown together. The protuberance at the point of union was as large as an egg, and the limb was bent like a bow. At the feet lay a skull of some enemy or slave. Several pipes and pendants were near the shoulders.

In the other graves Cowen made equally

In the other graves Cowen made equally interesting finds. It seems that this region was populated by a fairly intelligent people, and that the Serpent Mound was an object of worship. Near the graves is a large field in which broken implements, fragments of pottery, and burned stones give evidence of a pre historic village site.

The New York Times
Published: March 5, 1894

The Grave of a Giant.

Visitors go up on Pisgah almost every pleasant day. Mrs. Atwater, who is making some improvements, is still there and Mr. Cottrell of Mansfield is there and drives the team down occasionally for visitors. The Athens Historical society sent word to the mountain that they would visit it next Saturday. They claimed to know of an Indian grave on the top that they would open. The only Indian grave we ever knew of there says the Troy Gazette, was one on the south point of the mountain on the farm of Chas. W. Hooker. A very large thigh bone of a human being was dug up 45 years ago at that point near a spring.

It was of immense size and on its being shown to Dr. Theodore Wilder, he said it must have belonged to a man 7 feet high. "There were giants in those days.

Towanda Daily Review 10/25/1897

WISCONSIN MOUND OPENED.

Skeleton Found of a Man Over Nine Feet High with an Enormous Skull.

MAPLE CREEK, Wis., Dec. 19.—One of the three recently discovered mounds in this town has been opened. In it was found the skeleton of a man of gigantic size. The bones measured from head to foot over nine feet and were in a fair state of preservation. The skull was as large as a half bushel measure. Some finely tempered rods of copper and other relics were lying near the bones.

The mound from which these relics were taken is ten feet high and thirty feet long, and varies from six to eight feet in width.

The two mounds of lesser size will be excavated soon.

The New York Times

MAY BE RELATED
TO CARDIFF GIANT

Bones of a Human Skeleton Eleven Feet High Are Dug Up in Nevada.

WINNEMUCCA, Nev., Jan. 23.— Workmen engaged in digging gravel here today uncovered at a depth of about twelve feet a lot of bones, part of the skeleton of a gigantic human being.

Dr. Samuels examined them and pronounced them to be the bones of a man who must have been nearly eleven feet in height.

The metacarpal bones measure four and a half inches in length and are large in proportion. A part of the ulna was found and in its complete form would have been between seventeen and eighteen inches in length.

The remainder of the skeleton is being searched for.

The Saint Paul globe., January 24, 1904.

FIND GIANT INDIANS' BONES.

Workmen on Harlem Road Unearth Relics of Teekus Tribe.

Special to The New York Times.

KATONAH, N. Y., Sept. 6.—While a gang of men in the employ of the New York and Harlem Railroad were taking sand from an immense mound near Purdy's Station to-day to fill in an excavation, they unearthed several skeletons of unusual size.

The bones are believed to be those of Indians who once lived in this vicinity and belonged to a tribe that was led by the great Chief Teekus, from whom the Titicus Valley, now a part of the New York watershed, takes its name. Besides finding the bones, the workmen also exhumed a score or more of arrowheads, hatchets, and copper implements. It is believed that the large mound in which the relics were found was once the burying ground of the Teekus Indians. The last Indians were seen in the valley a short time after the Revolutionary War.

The bones found to-day were brought to Katonah and will be reinterred in the local cemetery.

The New York Times

Published: September 7, 1904

GIANTS' SKELETONS FOUND.

Cave in Mexico Gives Up the Bones of an Ancient Race.

Special to The New York Times.

BOSTON, May 3.—Charles C. Clapp, who has recently returned from Mexico, where he has been in charge of Thomas W. Lawson's mining interests, has called the attention of Prof. Agassiz to a remarkable discovery made by him.

He found in Mexico a cave containing some 200 skeletons of men each above eight feet in height. The cave was evidently the burial place of a race of giants who antedated the Aztecs. Mr. Clapp arranged the bones of one of these skeletons and found the total length to be 8 feet 11 inches. The femur reached up to his thigh, and the molars were big enough to crack a cocoanut. The head measured eighteen inches from front to back.

The New York Times
Published: May 4, 1908

STRANGE SKELETONS FOUND.

Indications That Tribe Hitherto Unknown Once Lived in Wisconsin.

Special to The New York Times.

MADISON, Wis., May 3.—The discovery of several skeletons of human beings while excavating a mound at Lake Delavan indicates that a heretofore unknown race of men once inhabited Southern Wisconsin. Information of the discovery was brought to Madison to-day by Maurice Morrissey, of Delavan, who came here to attend a meeting of the Republican State Central committee. Curator Charles E. Brown of the State Historical Museum will investigate the discoveries within a few days.

Upon opening one large mound at Lake Lawn farm, eighteen skeletons were discovered by the Phillips Brothers. The heads, presumably those of men, are much larger than the heads of any race which inhabit America to-day. From directly over the eye sockets, the head slopes straight back and the nasal bones protrude far above the cheek bones. The jaw bones are long and pointed, bearing a minute resemblance to the head of the monkey. The teeth in the front of the jaw are regular molars.

There were also found in the mounds the skeletons, presumably of women, which had smaller heads, but were similar in facial characteristics. The skeletons were embedded in charcoal and covered over with layers of baked clay to shed water from the sepulchre.

The New York Times
Published: May 4, 1912

The credit for the discovery goes to the expedition headed by Professor V. K. Morehead of Phillips-Andover Academy, and Professor A. B. Skinner of the American Indian Museum of New York, to which the skull of the horned Indian was shipped several days ago.

The expedition found at Athens one of the relics of lasting worth to the history of the Indian. The horned skull of this gigantic ancestor of the Iogans is probably the most spectacular of its discoveries but no less interesting is the assertion based on actual evidence that about 700 years ago Southern Tioga and Chemung counties and Northern Pennsylvania are inhabited by a race of men, perhaps Indians, and perhaps not, who were gigantic of stature and who lived only a short term of life, to prove the assertion of the scientists are the bones of 68 men of old taken from a single burying ground on the Murray Farm, which is situated on Tioga Point at the upper end of Queen Esther's flat. The average height of these men when the skeletons are assembled is seven feet, while many are much taller. Further evidence of their gigantic size is found in the remarkable large ribs or axes, hewed from stone, and in the graves with them and capable of being wielded only by a man of immense physical strength. When a man is 20 years old the sutures of the skull begin to knit. At 40 years they are completely joined. Thus scientists by examining a skull can tell you the age of the person. So Professor Skinner's reduction has been able to estimate with accuracy the age of these primeval men's death. At 40 one is a patriarch. Imagine the reverence with which one venerable gentleman, whose skull showed a man of nearly 70 years, must have been regarded. The average age of death, however, is estimated at 40 years. This premature death, says Professor Skinner and other members of his party, was almost wholly due to lack of medical knowledge — the practice of preventive medicine. Among tribes where the ravages of contagious disease was unchecked the lease of life was short. It was a wet, cold morning when E. Lord, who has been employed by Professor Skinner in Indian relic work for six years, uncovered the earth from one of the Murray Farm graves, and carefully picking away the soil beside an Indian skull, gave a yell which brought the other members of the party running to the grave.

"I've got 'orns," shouted Lord. Lord talks with an English accent. "'e in league with the devil." And sure enough, he had horns, a of solid bone which grew from the skull about an inch above the perfected skull and which gave every evidence of having been there since death. They were in no way attached to the skull. They were an integral

part of it. Then the scientists got out their notebooks and their cameras and searched their vocabulary for words meaningless to laymen, finally hitting upon "pithecanthropus erectus" as having just the right swing and describing the horns to a nicety.

Members of the expedition say that it is the first discovery of its kind on record of a valuable contribution to the history of the early races. The skull and what few bones were found in the grave with it have been shipped to the American Indian Museum. The party expects to find more horned heads further down the Susquehanna.

The party of scientists, which includes besides Professors Morehead and Skinner, Dr. George Donahue, Pennsylvania State Historian, E. O. Sodgen, a surveyor, and five other men who have had practical experience in digging up Indian burying grounds, left Cooperstown May 15, travelling down the Susquehanna in canoes. This river was chosen because it had never been worked scientifically before and promised rare treasures. It was agreed that whatever discoveries were made one-half of the relics should be given to a local institution or society, an agreement which has resulted in valuable acquisitions by the Athens Museum.

Sad to relate, the party met with an extremely cold reception in Broome county. They cannot altogether understand it, they say, but attribute it partly to the jealousy or antipathy of Binghamton Indian collectors. At East Windsor, however, they found an old shellbed where Indians once built their wigwams and cooked their fresh water clams, which were to be found in the river in abundance. Only the history of the Iroquois and Algonquins were studied. All the way down the Susquehanna and into Northern Pennsylvania the expedition found traces of Indian settlements with large camps at Great Bend and at Round Top, near Union.

And then came Waverly. The Murray farm was no less than a gold mine. In a few days the bones of 68 Indians had been taken from graves. First post holes were dug, then the land was surveyed and finally the work of digging was begun. It must be remembered that the early Indian had no metal tool, his combined spade, pick and hoe usually being the shoulder of some large animal. He dug a grave five feet deep and buried his dead, scattering a little earth over the bones. Another death and another Indian was tossed into the grave-stop the first.

It was convenient and a great labor saving device. In order not to waste room the dead Indian was hung in a tree until the flesh disappeared. Then the bones were tied in a bundle and tossed into the grave. Another method and shorter was to flex the body with the knees up to the chin. Only a few such burials were discovered in the grave.

The members of the Skinner expedition believe that the Murray burying ground is one of the largest that will be found. More graves might have been exhumed had the burying ground not run directly under a macadam road where excavations could not be made.

The party expects to conclude its labors near Baltimore, September 15.

STORY EXAGGERATED

Moorhead Expedition Did Not Find Giant Skeletons With Horns As Reported.

An article has been going the rounds of the press stating that the Moorhead Expedition which recently visited Athens and Waverly had unearthed at Athens giant skeletons with horns protruding from their skulls. Mr. Skinner of the expedition has just sent the following statement to the press, stating the true circumstances.

The statement follows: "Will you grant me the privilege of correcting the assertions of a news dispatch concerning a find made by our party and the alleged discovery of a mound near Sayre, Pa., in which the bones of men seven feet and more in height were unearthed? The dispatch further narrates the astounding fact that on some of the skulls, two inches above the perfectly formed forehead, were protuberances of bone, the inference being that those monsters were horned!

"As a matter of fact, over a month ago, our party excavated an Indian cemetery near Athens, Pa., which contained the skeletons of 57 perfectly normal individuals with the usual relics. One of the skeletons was covered by a deposit of deer antlers; hence, I suppose, the skull with horn on it!

"This report from Binghamton, coming a month or more later, furnishes an annoying example of the distortion of ordinary facts when spread by word of mouth, the more remarkable since full and truthful accounts were published by the local Athens paper at the time the find was made.

"ALANSON SKINNER,
"Susquehanna River Archaeological Expedition.
"In camp near Sunbury, Pa., July 14, 1916."

SKULLS OF GIANT CAVEMEN

many of these caves. At a depth of more than three feet he found the remains of several giant human skeletons, including an almost perfect skull which differed in many particulars from a modern specimen. When partly joined the largest skeleton was almost ten feet tall.

The New age magazine: Volume 18 Page 207 - 1913

GIANTS' BONES IN MOUND.

Scientists Unearth Relics of Indians Who Lived 700 Years Ago.

Special to The New York Times.

BINGHAMTON, July 13.—Profesor A. B. Skinner of the American Indian Museum, Professor W. K. Morehead of Phillips Andover Academy, and Dr. George Donohue, Pennsylvania State Historian, who have been conducting researches along the valley of the Susquehanna, have uncovered an Indian mound at Tioga Point, on the upper portion of Queen Esther's Flats, on what is known as the Murray farm, a short distance from Sayre, Penn., which promises rich additions to Indian lore.

In the mound uncovered were found the bones of sixty-eight men which are believed to have been buried 700 years ago. The average height of these men was seven feet, while many were much taller. Further evidence of their gigantic size was found in large celts or axes hewed from stone and buried in the grave. On some of the skulls, two inches above the perfectly formed forehead, were protuberances of bone. Members of the expedition say that it is the first discovery of its kind on record and a valuable contribution to the history of the early races.

The skull and a few bones found in one grave were sent to the American Indian Museum.

Chemung's Predecessors Huge Giants
Were Seven Feet Tall and Had Horns

WEDNESDAY, JULY 12, 1916.

One of the Most Remarkable Scientific Discoveries in History Made Here—Sixty-eight Skeletons of Men Living 700 Years Ago Unearthed Between Sayre and Waverly.—Men Were Old at Forty.

A QUEER FELLOW

He was seven feet in height.

Horns protruded from his skull.

His name (given him by the party) is "pithecanthropus erectus."

Perhaps he was an Indian, perhaps not.

At the age of thirty-five he was a tottering old gentleman; at forty, or earlier, he usually died.

Conjure up in your imagination a race of people 700 years old. Draw a mental picture of one of them. Make him seven feet tall and of perfect physique. Let him be strong but ignorant. Make him one of a race which at 35 years was growing old and which at 40 was near death. Finally give him horns, about an inch long, protruding from the skull about two inches above the ears. Such a man there was once and no further from Elmira than what is now the Murray farm in Sayre.

If you are just a mortal and human, picture those horns and say, "gee whiz." If you have the professional instinct, say that it is a perfect case of "pithecanthropus erectus" and jot it down mentally that it is the first discovery of its kind on record and one of the big Indian lore finds of recent years. The credit for the discovery goes to the expedition headed by Professor W. K. Moreland of Phillips-Andover Academy, and Professor A. B. Skinner of the American Indian Museum of New York, to which the skull of the horned Indian was shipped several days ago.

The expedition found at Sayre, contributions of lasting worth to the history of the Indian. The horned skull of this gigantic ancestor of the Tiogans is probably the most spectacular of its discoveries but no less interesting is the assertion based on actual evidence that about 700 years ago Southern Tioga and Chemung counties and Northern Pennsylvania were inhabited by a race of men, perhaps Indians, and perhaps not, who were gigantic of stature and who lived only a short term of life. To prove the assertion of the scientists are the bones of 68 men of old taken from a single burying ground on the Murray Farm, which is situated on Tioga Point at the upper end of Queen Esther's flat. The average height of these men when the skeletons are assembled is seven feet, while many are much taller. Further evidence of their gigantic size is found in the remarkable large celts or axes, hewed from stone, found in the graves with them and capable of being wielded only by a man of immense physical strength.

HOW AGE IS TOLD.

When a man is 20 years old, the seams of the skull begin to knit. At 80 years they are completely joined. Thus scientists by examining a skull will tell you the age of the person at death. So Professor Skinner's expedition has been able to estimate with accuracy the age of these primeval men's death. At 40 one was a patriarch. Imagine the reverence with which one venerable gentleman, whose skull showed a life of nearly 70 years, must have been regarded. The average age of death, however, is estimated at 40 years. This premature death, say Professor Skinner and other members of his party, was almost wholly due to lack of medical knowledge and the practice of preventive medicine. Among tribes where the ravages of contagious disease was unchecked the lease of life was short.

It was a wet, cold morning when R. H. Lord, who has been employed by Professor Skinner in Indian research work for six years, uncovered the earth from one of the Murray Farm graves, and carefully scooping away the soil beside an Indian skull, gave a yell which brought the 75 other members of the party running to the grave.

"He got 'orns," shouted Lord, who talks with an English accent. "E's in league with the devil."

HE SURELY HAD HORNS.

And sure enough, he had horns, horns of solid bone which grew straight out from the skull about two inches above the perfectly formed skull and which gave every evidence of having been there since birth. They were in no way attached to the skull. They were an integral part of it. Then the scientists got out their notebooks and their cameras and searched their vocabulary for words meaningless to layman, finally hitting upon "pithecanthropus erectus" as having just the right swing and describing the horns to a nicety.

Members of the expedition say that it is the first discovery of its kind on record of a valuable contribution to the history of the early races. The skull and what few bones were found in the grave with it have been shipped to the American Indian Museum. The party expects to find more horned heads further down the Susquehanna.

CAME FROM COOPERSTOWN

The party of scientists, which include, besides Professors Moreland and Skinner, Dr. George Donahue Pennsylvania State Historian, E. O. Sodgen, a surveyor, and ten other men who have had practical experience in digging up Indian burying grounds, left Cooperstown, May 15, traveling down the Susquehanna in canoes. This river was chosen because it had never been worked scientifically before and promised rare treasure. It was agreed that wherever discoveries were made one half of the relics should be given to a local institution or society, an agreement which has resulted in valuable acquisitions by the Sayre Museum.

Sad to relate, the party met with an extremely cold reception in Broome county. They cannot altogether understand it, they say, but attribute it partly to the jealousy or antipathy of Binghamton Indian collectors. At East Windsor, however, they found an old shellbed where Indians once built their wagwams and cooked their fresh water clams, which were to be found in the river in abundance. Only the history of the Iroquois and Algonquins was studied. All the way down the Susquehanna and into northern Pennsylvania the expedition found traces of Indian settlements with large camps at Great Bend and at Round Top, near Nichols.

And then came Waverly. The Murray farm was no less than a gold mine, in a few days the bones of 68 Indians had been taken from graves. First pouchholes were dug, then the land was surveyed and finally the work of digging was begun.

It must be remembered that the early Indian had no metal tool, his combined spade, pick and hoe usually being the shoulder of some large animal. He dug a grave five feet deep and buried his dead, scattering a little earth on the bones. Another death and another Indian was tossed into the grave atop the first.

It was convenient and a great labor saving device. In order not to waste room the dead Indian was hung in a tree until the flesh disappeared. Then the bones were tied in a bundle and tossed into the grave. Another method and shorter was to flex the body with the knees up to the chin. Only a few such burials were discovered in Sayre.

The members of the Skinner expedition believe that the Murray burying ground is one of the largest that will be found. More graves might have been exhumed had the burying ground not run directly under a macadam road where excavations could not be made. The party expects to conclude its labors near Baltimore September 15.

THURSDAY, JULY 13, 1916.

HUGE GIANTS
HERE ONCE

Conjure up in your imagination a race of people 700 years old. Draw a mental picture of one of them. Make him seven feet tall and of perfect physique. Let him be strong but ignorant. Make him one of a race which at 35 years was growing old and which at 40 was near death. Finally give him horns, about an inch long, protruding from the skull about two inches above the ears, such a man there was once and no further from Elmira than what is now the Murray farm near Athens, says the Elmira Star-Gazette.

If you are just a mortal and human, picture those horns and say, "gee whiz." If you have the professional instinct, say that it is a perfect case of "pithecanthropus erectus" and jot it down mentally that it is the first discovery of its kind on record and one of the big Indian lore finds of recent years.

139

GIANTS OF OTHER DAYS.

Recent Discoveries Near Serpent Mound, Ohio.

From The Indianapolis Journal

Farmer Warren Cowen of Hillsborough, Ohio, while fox hunting recently discovered several ancient graves. They were situated upon a high point of land in Highland County, Ohio, about a mile from the famous Serpent Mound, where Prof. Putnam of Harvard made interesting discoveries. As soon as the weather permitted, Cowen excavated several of these graves. The graves were made of large limestone slabs, two and a half to three feet in length and a foot wide. These were set on edge about a foot apart. Similar slabs covered the graves. A single one somewhat larger was at the head and another at the foot. The top of the grave was two feet below the present surface.

Upon opening one of the graves a skeleton upward of six feet in length was brought to light. There were a number of stone hatchets, beads, and ornaments of peculiar workmanship near the right arm. Several large flint spear and arrow heads among the ribs gave evidence that the warrior had died in battle.

In another grave was the skeleton of a man equally large. The right leg had been broken during life, and the bones had grown together. The protuberance at the point of union was as large as an egg, and the limb was bent like a bow. At the feet lay a skull of some enemy or slave. Several pipes and pendants were near the shoulders.

In the other graves Cowen made equally interesting finds. It seems that this region was populated by a fairly intelligent people, and that the Serpent Mound was an object of worship. Near the graves is a large field in which broken implements, fragments of pottery, and burned stones give evidence of a pre historic village site.

The New York Times

Published: March 5, 1594
Copyright @ The New York Times

NEW YORK TIMES 1925

GIANTS OF OTHER DAYS.

Recent Discoveries Near Serpent Mound, Ohio.

From The Indianapolis Journal.

Farmer Warren Cowen of Hillsborough, Ohio, while fox hunting recently discovered several ancient graves. They were situated upon a high point of land in Highland County, Ohio, about a mile from the famous Serpent Mound, where Prof. Putnam of Harvard made interesting discoveries. As soon as the weather permitted, Cowen excavated several of these graves. The graves were made of large limestone slabs, two and a half to three feet in length and a foot wide. These were set on edge about a foot apart. Similar slabs covered the graves. A single one somewhat larger was at the head and another at the foot. The top of the grave was two feet below the present surface.

Upon opening one of the graves a skeleton upward of six feet in length was brought to light. There were a number of stone hatchets, beads, and ornaments of peculiar workmanship near the right arm. Several large flint spear and arrow heads among the ribs gave evidence that the warrior had died in battle.

In another grave was the skeleton of a man equally large. The right leg had been broken during life, and the bones had grown together. The protuberance at the point of union was as large as an egg, and the limb was bent like a bow. At the feet lay a skull of some enemy or slave. Several pipes and pendants were near the shoulders.

In the other graves Cowen made equally interesting finds. It seems that this region was populated by a fairly intelligent people, and that the Serpent Mound was an object of worship. Near the graves is a large field in which broken implements, fragments of pottery, and burned stones give evidence of a pre-historic village site.

The New York Times

Published: March 5, 1894
Copyright © The New York Times

Beach Giant's Skull Unearthed By WPA Workers Near Victoria

Believed to Be Largest Ever Found in World; Normal Head Also Found

That Texas "had a giant on the beach" in the long ago appears probable from the large skull recently unearthed in a mound in Victoria County, believed to be the largest human skull ever found in the United States and possibly in the world.

Twice the size of the skull of a normal man, the fragments were dug up by W. Duffen, archaeologist, who is excavating the mound in Victoria County under a WPA project sponsored by the University of Texas. In the same mound and at the same level, a normal sized skull was found. The pieces taken from the mound were reconstructed in the WPA laboratory under supervision of physical anthropologists.

A study is being made to determine whether the huge skull was that of a man belonging to a tribe of extraordinary large men or whether the skull was that of an abnormal member of a tribe, a

case of giantism. Several large human body bones also have been unearthed at the site.

Marcus S. Goldstein, physical anthropologist, employed on the WPA project, formerly was an aide of Ales Hdrlicken, curator of the National Museum of Physical Anthropology.

Finds made through excavations in Texas are beginning to give weight to the theory that man lived in Texas 40,000 to 45,000 years ago, it is said.

STAMP SOCIETY MEETS

San Antonio Philatelic Society will hold its first meeting of 1940 at the Y. M. C. A. at 8:30 p. m.

Monday, when a bourse of rare stamps will be shown by collectors in this vicinity. New officers of the society are Norman H. Brock, president; B. A. Tur-

ner, vice president; L. F. Fiehl, secretary and treasurer, and Edward Albach, reporter. Both the president and vice president were re-elected.

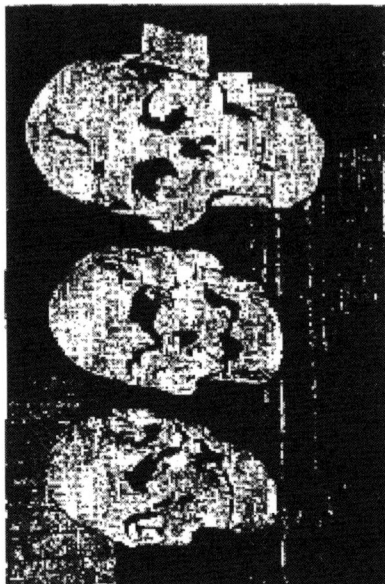

GIANT SKULL—Believed to be possibly the largest found in the world, the human skull shown on the right was recently unearthed in Victoria County by Texas University anthropologists. The other two are of normal size.

Ceremonial stones, scratched with the sign of the cross, show Spanish influence. Skull is of a giant Indian who was seven feet tall

Popular Science Oct 1932

Giant's Skeleton Found by Soviets

By the United Press

The skeleton of a giant, with a skull 33 inches around and a shin-bone 33 inches long, has been found in the Tien Mountains of Russian central Asia north of the Himalayas, the Russian official agency, Tass, reported yesterday in a broadcast.

FIND BONES IN INDIAN MOUNDS

Normal Professor and Students Excavate Historical Hills Near Stoddard

FIFTY SKELETONS UNEARTHED

Remains of Giant Aborigines Discovered; Weapons and Utensils Are Buried

FIND SKELETON TEN FEET TALL

Irish Excavators Dig Up Prehistoric Giant's Bones.

[By the Associated Press.]

LONDON, April 2.—According to a dispatch published here today, the skeleton of a person who had been apparently ten feet in height has been found at Dysart, county Louth, Ireland. The skull of the giant, supposed to have been buried in prehistoric times, measured eighteen inches from the crown of the head to the chin.

FIND OLD GRAVES

Skeletons of Giant Warriors Unearthed in France.

Men Who Lived 25,000 Years Ago Believed to Have Died Fighting—Arrow Found in Head of One.

The discovery of 25,000-year-old

When Giants Roamed Earth

The past was more prolific in the production of giants than the present. In 1830 one of these giants, who was exhibited at Rouen, was ten feet high, and the giant Galabre, brought from Arabia to Rome in the time of Claudius Caesar, was the same height. Fannum, who lived in the time of Eugene II, was eleven and one-half feet in height.

The Chevalier Scrog in his journey to the Peak Teneriffe found in one of the caverns of that mountain the head of a giant who had sixty teeth and who was not less than fifteen feet high. The giant Faragus, slain by Orlando, the nephew of Charlemagne, according to reports, was twenty-eight feet high. In 1814 near St. Gernad was found the tomb of the giant Isolent, who was not less than thirty feet high. In 1590 near Rouen was found a skeleton whose head held a bushel of corn and which was nineteen feet in height. The giant Bacrt was twenty-two feet high.

In 1623 near the castle in Dauphine a tomb was found thirty feet long, sixteen feet wide and eight feet high, on which were cut in gray stone the wards, "Kentolochus Rex." The skeleton was found entire and measured twenty-five and one-fourth feet high, ten feet across the shoulders and five feet from breastbone to the back.

But France is not the only country where giant skeletons have been unearthed. Near Palermo, Sicily, in 1516, was found the skeleton of a giant thirty feet high. Near Magrino, on the same island, in 1816, was found the skeleton of a giant of thirty feet whose head was the size of a hogshead and each tooth weighed five ounces.

abroad, a noted doctor, quench what he considered tion, went down one eveni parson's grave in the chur the sea, and, sitting on th lit his pipe as the clock stru is true also that a succeedir er professed to have heard inexplicable noises procee the attic in which the su curred, but he observed:

"As long as he keeps don't mind." Some agnostic ed folk may have more n others.

Personally, I have heard many stories of what has b the right side of nature, nc for publication, but as sti periences by friends and ances whose honesty and go have no reason whatever to

A lady I know was resi her uncle and aunt. The dangerously ill. One even and niece were sitting in downstairs in which was an father's clock which had n Suddenly withou

Georgia's Sand-Dunes Yield Startling Proof of a Prehistoric Race of Giants

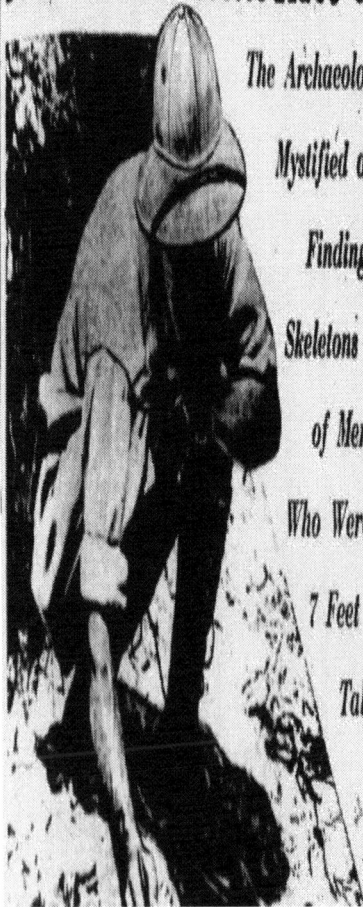

The Archaeologists Were Mystified at Finding Skeletons of Men Who Were 7 Feet Tall

Science is Stumped By Strange Mummies in Utah

No Possible Explanation Yet to Account for the Red Headed, Wavy Haired, Perhaps White, Race in America, Thousands of Years Before the Indians or Even the Cliff Dwellers

The Type of Thoroughly Explored Utah Cliff Dwelling, Deep Beneath Which Were Found the Mummies and Remains of the Mysterious Lost Red-Headed American Race

By Dr. W. H. Ballou.

A Tragic Prehistoric Woman, the Last Representative of the Lost Red-Headed Race, Left Unburied Beside the Tombs of Her People.

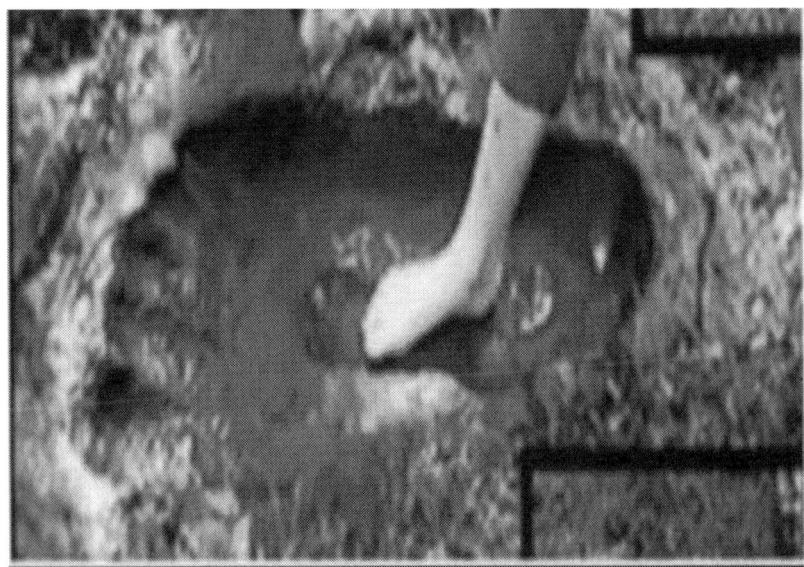

When Giants Roamed Earth

The past was more prolific in the production of giants than the present. In 1830 one of these giants, who was exhibited at Rouen, was ten feet high, and the giant Galabra, brought from Arabia to Rome in the time of Claudius Caesar, was the same height. Fannum, who lived in the time of Eugene II, was eleven and one-half feet in height.

The Chevalier Scrog in his journey to the Peak Teneriffe found in one of the caverns of that mountain the head of a giant who had sixty teeth and who was not less than fifteen feet high. The giant Faragus, slain by Orlando, the nephew of Charlemagne, according to reports, was twenty-eight feet high. In 1814 near St. Gernad was found the tomb of the giant isolent, who was not less than thirty feet high. In 1590 near Rouen was found a skeleton whose head held a bushel of corn and which was nineteen feet in height. The giant Bacrt was twenty-two feet high.

In 1623 near the castle in Dauphine a tomb was found thirty feet long, sixteen feet wide and eight feet high, on which were cut in gray stone the wards, "Kentolochus Rex." The skeleton was found entire and measured twenty-five and one-fourth feet high, ten feet across the shoulders and five feet from breastbone to the back.

But France is not the only country where giant skeletons have been unearthed. Near Palermo, Sicily, in 1516, was found the skeleton of a giant thirty feet high. Near Magrino, on the same island, in 1816, was found the skeleton of a giant of thirty feet whose head was the size of a hogshead and each tooth weighed five ounces.

abroad, a noted doctor, quench what he considered tion, went down one eveni parson's grave in the chur the sea, and, sitting on th lit his pipe as the clock stru is true also that a succeedir er professed to have heard inexplicable noises proceed the attic in which the su curred, but he observed:

"As long as he keeps r don't mind." Some agnostic ed folk may have more n others.

Personally, I have heard many stories of what has b the right side of nature, no for publication, but as str periences by friends and ances whose honesty and go have no reason whatever to

A lady I know was resl her uncle and aunt. The i dangerously ill. One even and niece were sitting in downstairs in which was an father's clock which had n for years. Suddenly, withor certained cause, the weigh

Charity Machine a Wonder

"A charity machine," said the sailor, "stands in front of the house of Edison Murphy of Croydon. Any tramp that comes along can get a cent out of the machine.

"The tramps don't believe their eyes at first. They stand and look at the charity machine in a knowing way. They say to themselves that they ain't green, and it's no use tryin' to do them.

"But there the big, cast iron instrument stands, and it states plain and direct on the dial of it that any ... If he turns the handle a while. Then he turns with the left hand. At fifty he stops to rest, and with a grunt he wipes the beads from his brow. Finally out drops a cent.

"The tramp grins. He thinks he'll turn ten hundred times, and get ten cents for two beers. He is pretty tired; though, by the time he's turned 500 times, and, besides, the morning is pretty well gone now. So he stops at the five hundred. He goes off with five coppers, rubbin' his arms. His arms'll be stiff next day.

"Hard-earned coppers! Edison Murphy calls his invention a charity machine, but there's not much charity

When Giants Roamed Earth

The past was more prolific in the production of giants than the present. In 1830 one of these giants, who was exhibited at Rouen, was ten feet high, and the giant Galabra, brought from Arabia to Rome in the time of Claudius Caesar, was the same height. Fannum, who lived in the time of Eugene II, was eleven and one-half feet in height.

The Chevalier Scrog in his journey to the Peak Teneriffe found in one of the caverns of that mountain the head of a giant who had sixty teeth and who was not less than fifteen feet high. The giant Faragus, slain by Orlando, the nephew of Charlemagne, according to reports, was twenty-eight feet high. In 1814 near St. Gernad was found the tomb of the giant Isolent, who was not less than thirty feet high. In 1590 near Rouen was found a skeleton whose head held a bushel of corn and which was nineteen feet in height. The giant Baert was twenty-two feet high.

In 1623 near the castle in Dauphine a tomb was found thirty feet long, sixteen feet wide and eight feet high, on which were cut in gray stone the wards, "Kentolochus Rex." The skeleton was found entire and measured twenty-five and one-fourth feet high, ten feet across the shoulders and five feet from breastbone to the back.

But France is not the only country where giant skeletons have been unearthed. Near Palermo, Sicily, in 1516, was found the skeleton of a giant thirty feet high. Near Magrino, on the same island, in 1816, was found the skeleton of a giant of thirty feet whose head was the size of a hogshead and each tooth weighed five ounces.

Printed in Great Britain
by Amazon